PRAISE FOR MATT BROWN

"Upon meeting Matt Brown, I was struck by his kind demeanor, positive attitude, and amazing willpower. His continued perseverance is incredible."

RAY BOURQUE, *Olympian and former captain of the Boston Bruins*

"Matt's courage and willpower to stay positive in the face of adversity is something I truly admire. Matt is one of the toughest kids I've ever met, and his motto to 'Never Quit' sticks with me. The entire hockey community is proud to call him one of our own."

PATRICE BERGERON, *NHL player and alternate captain for the Boston Bruins*

"Matt's spirit, perseverance, and attitude are unmatched. I know there is nothing that he will not be able to accomplish with his positive mindset and the unwavering support of not only the hockey community, but those who are fortunate enough to meet him along the way."

JIM CRAIG, *former NHL goaltender, 1980 Olympic gold medalist, and president of Gold Medal Strategies*

"Attending college as a full-time student and living in a dorm with your peers [as a spinal cord injury survivor] is an undertaking that able-bodied people can't fully understand due to the complexities and difficulties involved. Matt's story garnered a lot of attention and I'm grateful, along with every other spinal cord injury survivor, that he has chosen to use the spotlight that was placed on him to help create awareness."

TRAVIS ROY, *spinal cord injury survivor, philanthropist, and former ice hockey player for Boston University*

"Matt Brown is a five-time Boston Marathon finisher, which by itself is a feat to be extremely proud of. Like many Marathon competitors, Matt competes with a story, and his story is one of grit and guts and determination."

DAVE McGILLIVRAY, *race director of the Boston Marathon*

"*Line Change* brings to life Matt's remarkable attitude, courage, and selflessness. You'll discover that even when feeling helpless, you can still be helpful. I would recommend this book to every father, mother, sister, brother, teammate, celebrity, and friend, as it shares some thought-provoking and compelling life lessons."

CLEON DASKALAKIS, *retired goaltender for the Boston Bruins 1984-1987 and president of Celebrity Marketing*

"Matt's undeniable spirit as he grinds toward his recovery shows how much determination he has, which he had both before the accident and now."

TIM SWEENEY, *Olympian and NHL player for the Boston Bruins*

"When I'm asked about Matt Brown, the first thing that comes to mind is his sense of humor. His attitude and outlook on life is a true inspiration to me, and should be to all."

SHAWN THORNTON, *former NHL player for the Boston Bruins, Florida Panthers, and Anaheim Ducks, and founder of the Shawn Thornton Foundation*

"Over the years, I've followed Matt's story of hard work and dedication. Matt is living proof of the Team Hoyt motto, 'Yes You Can!'"

DICK HOYT, *marathoner, triathlete, father of Rick Hoyt, and half of famed father/son running duo*

"Matt Brown personifies everything good and positive in life. His determination, attitude, and approach to every challenge has redefined courage and gratitude. His remarkable story is an inspiration to us all."

SUSAN WORNICK, *former reporter and anchor, WCVB-TV Boston*

"Attitude is a choice we all make every minute of every day. Matt Brown's example of positive attitude through tremendously difficult circumstances is an inspiration. There is great value in knowing that no matter what the obstacles we face, success is possible."

KARL MECKLENBURG, *former NFL linebacker for the Denver Broncos, NFL All Pro, keynote speaker, and award-winning author*

"As a Boston native with a long career in the sports world, I have followed Matt Brown's story closely. His spirit, grit, and determination summarize what it takes to be a New England athlete. I am proud to consider him my peer."

STEVE DeOSSIE, *former NFL linebacker for the Dallas Cowboys, New York Giants, New York Jets, and New England Patriots*

"Matt Brown is a true New Englander and true inspiration for all of us. You will love this book."

BUTCH STEARNS, *Boston TV and radio sportscaster*

"Matt Brown's story has redefined the phrase 'Never Quit' for me. It means not giving up, every minute, every day until the moment he places his two feet upon the ground and walks again, and then some."

TODD RUCCI, *former NFL guard for the New England Patriots 1993-2001 and collegiate athlete for Pennsylvania State University*

"Matt's is a story of strength and courage and will to succeed, and I'm so happy that Todd Civin is bringing his story to all of us. You'll love this story!"

DALE ARNOLD, *New England sportscaster and host of Boston Bruins broadcasts on NESN*

"Matt Brown's book is an inspirational account of a courageous young man who maintains a positive attitude and refuses to quit. Matt is a ray of sunshine, and by reading *Line Change* he will forever be in your presence."

GEORGE S. USEVICH, *Principal Emeritus, Norwood High School*

"Patriots owner Robert Kraft once said, 'There are very few people on this earth who can turn adversity into an advantage.' Matt Brown is one of those people. *Line Change* is a must-read. Matt Brown teaches you not only how to face adversity, but how to conquer it."

STEVE BURTON, *sports director for WBZ-TV*

"Matt Brown's journey demonstrates a spirit and a positive determination to not only heal and overcome physical injury, but enables him to move his life in a direction that puts him squarely in the company of any other Boston-area athlete, both past and present. We consider him a hero."

LEIGH RADATZ, *daughter of Red Sox Hall of Famer, Dick "The Monster" Radatz*

LINE CHANGE

A True Story of Resilience in the Face of Adversity

MATT BROWN

with Todd Civin

www.mascotbooks.com

Line Change: A True Story of Resilience in the Face of Adversity

Cover Photograph by Edodge Photography

For more information, please contact:
Mascot Books
620 Herndon Parkway #320
Herndon, VA 20170
info@mascotbooks.com

CPSIA Code: PRFRE1118A
Library of Congress Control Number: 2018912449
ISBN-13: 978-1-64307-210-4

Printed in Canada

To Mom, Dad, and Kelley—this journey has been a roller coaster, but your love and support has always been consistent. We will get there. Love.

CONTENTS

FOREWORD

Andrew Ference

National Hockey League player, 2001–2017

During my NHL career, I've met a number of extremely tough, very impressive people. I've had the pleasure of meeting NHL Hall of Famers, top Ultimate Fighting Championship fighters, Special Forces Green Berets, Olympic champions, and this kid from Norwood, Massachusetts, named Matt Brown.

I first met Matt a few months after his accident. After one of our games, he was down in the bowels of the TD Garden with a mutual friend of ours, Sgt. Lucas Carr (RLTW). I knew Matt's story from seeing it on the Boston news stations and from hearing Patrice Bergeron talk about visiting him in hospital. I knew about his situation, but I had no idea who he actually was.

I can't recall exactly how our first conversation went, but I remember walking home after the game having learned the following:

a) This kid was surrounded by really good friends and family.

b) Matt was pretty excited about his "smokin' hot" girlfriend.

c) He was polite enough to refrain from giving his honest opinion about what our team and individual players could improve upon, but forward enough to make sure that I knew that *he* knew.

d) I had been invited to his family's house in Norwood.

e) He has an infectious smile and laugh and would never waste an opportunity to deliver a solid jab to one of his buddies.

f) This was a guy I wanted to get to know a bit better.

After taking him up on the invitation to his home in Norwood a few days later, my family and I quickly understood why a teenager that had been dealt such a tough hand could be seemingly doing so well. I saw a home filled with friendship, laughter, and a deep love from his mom, dad, and sister. Matt was surrounded by friends in his basement, who were not in bereavement but (in typical hockey player fashion) making fun of each other and cracking locker-room jokes. Even in a room full of teenage friends, Matt made sure to welcome my family into his home and was a gracious host. His family was in the eye of a storm, trying to figure out their new normal, but they still had time to deliver incredible hospitality to Matt's friends and my family. During our visit, we made an addition to a staircase full of handprints, each hand representing a person who had touched the Brown family's life over the years. It is a wall that is filled with memories and friendship, and I am honored to be a part of it.

Since our initial meetings, I have seen Matt move through life with vigor and determination, which flat-out inspires me. I witnessed him finish school, find some independence, chase love and dreams, run marathons with Lucas, endure countless hours of rehabilitation … all which, frankly, take a thousand-fold effort due to his paralysis. Through it all, I have never heard a single complaint from him about the challenges of it. This attitude brings me to a quick story that sums up my admiration for this kid from Norwood.

When we won the Stanley Cup in 2011, we had a player-of-the-game jacket, which would not necessarily go to the "star" of the game, but rather to a guy who made a huge play or sacrificed himself for the betterment of the team. It was a coveted award after every playoff win and worn with honor, in all its ugliness, because it represented the grit, fortitude, and selflessness that it takes to win NHL playoff games. That jacket is framed in the Bruins locker room as a symbol of that team's incredible determination to bring the Cup back to Beantown after an absence of nearly four decades.

The jacket sparked a bit of a tradition as we rolled through the Stanley Cup playoffs in 2013. The new player-of-the-game jacket was United States Army Rangers garb, supplied by Matt's and my mutual buddy, Lucas Carr. The jacket would be rightfully worn by some tough competitors that year, including Bergeron, who would play through the pain of broken ribs, a punctured lung, and countless other bumps and bruises to lead us to the Cup finals against Chicago. Sadly, we lost in Game 6 that year and were unable to bring another Cup home to Boston. Even in defeat, there was an incredible sense of pride in not only being a part of that team but also a son of the City of Boston. We worked hard to make our fans proud, and we always made that our priority, rather than worrying about wins and losses.

But without a finals win, our jacket was without a proper home. It had been on the shoulders of overtime heroes and corner warriors who had led us close to another Cup. I was fortunate enough to deliver it to the only rightful recipient we could think of following the sounding of the final horn. It was someone who had shown incredible determination, inspired others to be better, and attacked life with positivity no matter the challenges that were thrown his way. When I presented the jacket to Matt Brown, I am sure I didn't articulate just how worthy a recipient he was then and remains today. The jacket is not just a jacket: it represents a deep respect and pride that I and many others have toward Matt. We know it can't be easy, no matter how big his smile or how sharp his jokes. This kid doesn't even realize the lesson in perseverance that he has delivered to so many people, including a ton of guys pulling on NHL jerseys each night. Knowing Matt has made me a better person. I am proud to call him a friend.

CHAPTER 1

A Thousand Sunsets

The day should have been one of the highlights of my brief high school hockey career. We were about to take on our nemesis, Weymouth High, at the Pilgrim Arena in Hingham, and I had accomplished my goal of skating with the varsity. After a season and a half of cutting my teeth with the junior varsity squad, I had recently been blessed with the honor of a call-up. For the remainder of my sophomore year, I'd be lacing them up and skating with the big boys. Every time I hit the ice marked a memorable day in my life, but this day was one I would certainly never, ever forget.

If that wasn't enough, just the day before, I had finally mustered up the courage to ask Meghan to be my girlfriend, and we had plans to hang out after the game. Our plans were nothing really definitive; we'd probably watch a movie or something—just regular teenage plans, but our first official "date" nonetheless. Though I thought about her endlessly each night and nearly every waking moment in between, once the alarm clock sounded that Saturday morning, I thought of nothing but the other love of my life: hockey.

My team had skated against our longtime and much-hated rival Walpole the week before, and most of us had decided to get crazy haircuts, bleaching our hair a fiery shade of blond before hitting the ice against the Rebels. Meghan hated the look with a passion, so I decided to traipse down to Charlie's Barber Shop the morning before we headed for Hingham, with no plan of telling her that I had cleaned myself up just to make her happy.

Charlie's shop is right in the center of Norwood, and it is where my dad and I have gone to get cleaned up ever since I was a kid. It is your typical, small-town barber shop with décor that makes it feel like it's straight out of an old TV western. There are two big black leather chairs in the middle of the shop, surrounded by an occasional pile of multicolored hair that builds up between customers. Steve is my regular barber, and he always hooks me up with a cut, quite a bit more conventional than the blond Mohawk I was sporting when I entered the shop.

While I waited for Steve, I thumbed through a dated edition of *Sports Illustrated*, which featured former hometown hero-gone-sour Manny Ramirez and spoke of his trade to the Dodgers. Of far more interest to me, however, was a story highlighting the 2009 NHL playoffs. I knew the ultimate outcome of the Stanley Cup, since the magazine was six months old, but I still enjoyed reading about the first-round series, which pit the top-seeded Boston Bruins against the utterly vile and worthless Bleu, Blanc, and Rouge of the Montreal Canadians. There is no greater rivalry in sport, in my opinion, and I enjoyed every word written about the way Bergeron, Lucic, and Thornton had taken care of those pukes from St. Catherine Street. As Steve swept up the remnants of hair left by his previous client, he called me over to the chair and laughed at my haircut as I whipped off my hat and hood. He shook his head slightly as if to say, "I'm a barber, Matt. Not a magician," but I had faith that he could restore me to my previous good looks. We participated in the normal barbershop banter about the weather and things going on at school. Steve's not a big hockey fan, so I didn't talk about it more than to mention the upcoming game. Despite the fact that Steve claimed he couldn't perform the impossible, he worked his magic on my golden locks and had me cleaned up in no time. Meghan was sure to be quite a bit happier with my well-groomed appearance.

Later that afternoon, the team arrived at good ol' Norwood High and boarded the bus. We were dressed in our traditional blue and gold sweatshirts with our names and numbers embroidered on the back, flanked by a pair of crossed hockey sticks. The bus was scheduled to leave Norwood between 2:30 and 3:00 p.m. to get us down to Hingham by about 3:30 p.m. for warm up time. After a surprisingly quiet bus ride during which the team seemed to be deep in thought, we filed off the bus. I dragged my bag and sticks into the Pilgrim Arena and walked through the doors of the tiny locker room. Every time we played at Pilgrim, we marveled at the fact that we were seemingly right on top of one another as the changing area is incredibly undersized. Everyone had their jump suits on, and we headed out to the parking lot to engage in a couple of pre-game sprints and to stretch. We would normally warm up in a hallway between the locker room and the rink, but at the Hingham Rink, the fans stand in that hallway, so there was no place for our pregame ritual.

I was the last one to leave the cold parking lot following the stretch. I stopped and reflected for a few seconds, gazing at the sun as the rest of the team hustled back into the teeny locker room. It wasn't as weird then as it seems to me now, in retrospect. I've seen a thousand sunsets, and this one was no different than any of the others. It stands out in my mind as a moment in time that's been indelibly etched into my brain. Was that moment foreshadowing the fact that I'd never again be able to see the world in quite the same bright, shiny way as I did before? Was it some sort of metaphor to teach me that although I was about to enter the darkest period of my life, the sun would someday shine again? Or was it none of the above and just a temporary delay so that I didn't have to return to that miniscule locker room packed with twenty blue and gold sardines?

I made my way into the locker room and started to get undressed, being especially careful not to accidently rub my bare skin against the guy next to me in the tight quarters. (Nothing spells awkward quite like finding yourself "cheek to cheek" with one of your line mates.) I've long been sort of a clown, and I started joking around with the boys as a way to keep everyone loose. We were all pretty relaxed but, at the same time, focused on the game ahead. I was in a corner, surrounded by a bunch of dented lockers in the visitors changing room. Our bags were literally on top of one another, so there wasn't much room to get our gear on.

I sat on the wooden bench and started to put on my shin pads. Breaking from my normal routine, I carelessly put the right one on first. That never happens. We are all very superstitious, doing things the exact same way before every game: left leg first, right leg second. Left sock first, right sock second. Left skate first, right skate second. So, putting my pads on incorrectly was weird to me. However, I'm truly not much of a believer in the paranormal, so I played it off as nerves about going up against a powerhouse like Weymouth, but much like my casual gaze into the sun, I have occasionally wondered if it was a sign that things just weren't quite normal that day.

After what seemed like forever, we left the locker room and charged onto the ice for our pregame skate. After the customary laps around our end of the ice, the game finally began, and I was on the third line. After a few shifts, it was clear that our line wasn't playing very well, and unfortunately I was a big part of our problem. It's a funny thing in sports that although your skill set never changes from game to game, there are times your level of emotion is a bit off and the chemistry between line mates suffers. I'm not sure if it was a case of nerves and beginning the game less than engaged, but we all were a bit slow and tentative; we were getting beat to every loose puck. Weymouth was buzzing around us, and we were just not moving our feet. For that period, they seemed bigger, faster, and stronger—they clearly dominated the first fifteen minutes of play. Weymouth was one of the better teams in the state, but it was certainly a team we felt we could beat if we brought our A-game. Unfortunately, I'd say the first period our game was a big, fat C+.

We left the ice after the first fifteen minutes down only 2–1, but it seemed a whole lot worse. We left the bench, heads down, knowing we had survived a terrible display of hockey as we made our way towards that elfin locker room. Coach Clifford was not pleased, to say the least, and began reaming us out even before we made it out of the runway. He was partly pissed off for real at our sub-par effort and in part just trying to light a fire under our lackluster asses. Our line was benched towards the end of the first period as coach sent us a message loud and clear that we were flat. In the next period, he tried to mix things up a bit by sitting two of us out, while one would play a shift. Then all three of us would sit again before he'd tap one of us on the shoulder to hop over the boards for another shift. He was trying to mix-and-match, hoping he could discover a combination that would make something happen. Hockey is a lot like chemistry class: it often takes some experimentation to find the right formula to ignite a chemical interaction. A bit of hustle and a lucky bounce can suddenly combust and change the momentum of a game.

My line mates were Connor Mahon and Danny Wiseman. Danny was a freshman who normally played defense. During the hockey season, we were all like brothers, each knowing what the other was thinking and what move our line mates were about to make. The more you play together, the more you begin to anticipate and the easier the game becomes. I don't know what it was that day, but our line was out of sync and, honestly, we appeared to be skating with concrete blocks on our feet.

We sat in the locker room and planned what we needed to do to change the momentum of the game. If we continued to play like this, Weymouth would mop up the ice with us cleaner than the Zamboni could. The second period began, and I was still parked on the bench, stick gripped tightly in my gloves as I watched the action go up and down the ice. Every once in a while, I'd glance at the coach out of the corner of my eye to see if it was my turn to get back in, almost willing him to call my number. A few shifts went by, and finally I got the nod, but still not with my original line. About halfway through the period, the coach turned and looked at us with fire in his eyes. He leaned over to Connor, Danny, and me and said, "Now, go do something."

That was all we needed to hear. Hoping to produce the lift the team needed, I jumped the boards fired up, intent on doing just what Coach Clifford ordered. Our bench was on the other end of the rink, so I gained speed as I chased the puck towards our defensive zone. I felt like the entire bench had their eyes on me, knowing that I wanted to make something happen. From a hockey standpoint, I was totally out of position as a forward behind our own net, but I was a bit embarrassed about the way we played, and the way I had played, in the first period and was hell-bent on making up for it. I was hoping that my hustle would provide a spark to elevate our otherwise lackluster play.

My love for hockey was unparalleled, and yet none of my affection for the sport would have been possible without the sacrifice of my parents. As any kid who has played the game knows, the commitment of hockey parents is an absolute must if you have any desire to play the sport. There's nothing fun for a parent about leaving a warm bed at 3:45 a.m. in order to get their kid to school for morning practice. Every other week, either Mom or Dad would rise to the blaring of their alarm clock, wipe the sleep from their eyes, throw on a sweatshirt over their pajama top, and haul my uncooperative ass to the bus. We were lucky that my parents and the parents of teammates Mark, Kyle, and Peter would split carpool duties so that the early morning sounding of reveille was only an occasional occurrence for each set of parents.

We do not have a hockey rink in Norwood, so we would practice in Walpole in the morning and at Hyde Park almost every day after school. In both cases we needed to take a bus to the rink. For morning practice, the bus would pick us up at the high school at 4:30 a.m. We only had morning practice once or twice a week, and though it sucked getting up that early, once you got into the locker room with the boys it was pure nirvana. We would hit the ice at 5:15 a.m. and skate until about 6:45 a.m. Walpole had six or seven locker rooms, but we would squeeze our close-knit crew all into one locker room. Though only members of the hockey fraternity might understand this next statement, there was nothing better than showering with the boys after practice. It was teenage comradery and team-building at its finest. We would slap each other with wet towels, talk about hockey and girls, and bond as a team.

After practice, we packed everything up, got back on the bus, and were dropped off at school in time for class. We got out of school about 2:20 p.m., to either workout in the weight room or watch a film. By 3:30 or 4:00, the bus would take us back to the rink to skate until 5:00 or 6:00 before we grabbed something to eat and did homework. We were almost entirely together night and day throughout the season.

I gathered the puck in somewhere around the face-off dot, and as I was circling around the net, the puck came off my stick and ricocheted off the end board. After it bounced off the back wall, it nestled between my feet. I looked down to regain control of the wobbling puck and sensed a Weymouth player converging on me. He bumped me from behind—not a vicious hit, just a bump—but I lost my footing and the top of my head smashed into the boards. Down in a heap, I slumped onto the ice as the sun set slowly behind the Pilgrim Arena.

CHAPTER 2

A Clean Hockey Play

Luckily, I've never had to endure a near-death experience, and so I am not privy to whether or not life truly passes before your eyes as is often reported. I can tell you, however, without a speck of doubt, that although it wasn't a near-death situation, during the moments I lay motionless on the sheet of ice behind my own net at the Pilgrim Arena in Hingham, a virtual scrapbook of my memories, like the DVD of my life, fast-forwarded through my mind.

My thoughts instantly catapulted me back to my Norwood Mites days, when I was first introduced to hockey, skating with many of the same guys that make up the varsity and junior varsity (JV) squads today. I witnessed a younger, less filled-out version of me, skating up and down the ice in my blue and gold Norwood Nuggets sweater. I wore the number two at the time in honor of my uncle, Pete Brown. Pete is a cousin on my mother's side. A little-known fact in the annals of Brown family lore is that Mom's maiden name was Brown, as well. We've often believed that Mom and Dad were alphabetically destined to marry as Mom, Susan Brown, sat in front of Dad, Mike Brown, throughout middle school and into high school. For those of you wondering, my slightly off-center personality does not in any way indicate that my parents are actually blood-related to one another, though I'd be lying if I told you it hadn't crossed my mind.

Prior to the start of my sophomore season, I played "midget-minor" hockey. I credit this half season of hockey to the relative success

I had in preparing myself for the upcoming season. I kept getting better and stronger as I geared up for my high school season. On average, we usually only had nine or ten guys show up for our midget games, so this meant we skated only two lines. This resulted in about thirty minutes of ice time for each of us during the thirty-six-minute game. We'd double or even triple shift, before taking a one-minute breather and hitting the ice again. There were games that we only had one sub, resulting in an exhausting half hour of up-and-down-the-ice hockey. During this half season, I could feel myself getting better with moving the puck and increasing in confidence. Many nights, we'd hit the ice and find ourselves playing ten against twenty. In many ways, this allowed us to play the role of underdog every night and caused us to play with a bit of a chip on our collective shoulders. We skated and worked hard to win every battle, and despite our roster deficiencies, we advanced all the way to the state semi-finals at the midget level.

Many of my teammates on the JV team also played as midgets, so despite our small numbers, we succeeded at developing a hard-working core of players that formed the nucleus of our Norwood JV team. Following varsity tryouts, my friend Kyle and I found ourselves in the same boat, both getting cut from varsity on the same day and each being relegated by the JV squad. After overcoming the initial shock of getting cut, we commiserated with each other and accepted the fact that as long as we were playing hockey, it really didn't matter who we were playing for. We loved the sport and felt complete whenever we were chasing the hard rubber disc up and down the ice.

During the JV games, the varsity team would watch us play from the stands before hitting the locker room to change. Coach Clifford was there, and I'd bust my ass during the game to get him to notice my effort and commitment. In between practices and games, I'd shoot about 500 weighted pucks a day in my backyard and do push-ups and sit-ups. After our practices or games ended, the JV coach would often come in and tell a few of us that we were staying behind to skate with the varsity team. This was a dream come true. I would play in a game, score a couple goals, and then practice with many of my friends and the varsity team. My hard work was finally starting to pay off. It was so rewarding to see that I was being noticed.

I credit my uncle Pete for introducing me to hard work, diligence, and to my backyard regimen, which really made me much stronger. He was responsible for initially getting me on skates, and due to his success in the game, I looked up to him as a mentor. Uncle Pete and I would talk hockey for hours on end. He was my idol, and I loved to hear stories about how his 1972 Norwood High team won a state championship. I dreamed that someday, while I was wearing the Norwood High sweater, that I too would reach similar heights.

Uncle Pete went on to skate for Boston University. Pete was elected to the Terrier Hall of Fame and was drafted by both the Atlanta Flames of the NHL and the New England Whalers of the now-defunct World Hockey Association. I like to think that I inherited my hockey DNA from Uncle Peter, though he clearly dove into the gene pool quite a few more times than I did. Legend has it that Pete was truly a gifted hockey player. It's common in sports to fall in love with a uniform number in order to honor and idolize the player who wore it. I continued to "don the deuce" during my JV season at Norwood, but when I got called up to the varsity team, the number was already in the possession of an upperclassmen. It's no secret that seniority reigns in high school sports, so I had to give up my beloved number two. The day I was summoned to play on the varsity squad, Coach Clifford told me to meet him in the equipment room. As I walked in, he tossed me a sweater with "3" embroidered on the back. Not that I had much of a choice, but I actually liked the way three looked, so the transition was not very difficult.

I didn't know then that "three" would become more than just a number to me and would ultimately become synonymous with my name. Though obviously not even in the same stratosphere as the following players, you know you're somewhat of a legend when your number replaces your name: 4 will always be Bobby Orr; 99, Wayne

Gretzky; and 77, via 7, Ray Bourque. In the history of Norwood High, 3 would ultimately become equated with injured athlete Matt Brown.

Not long after being called up to play with the varsity team, I was inserted into the lineup whenever we played our rival, Walpole. I had played a bit near the end of the second period during the game prior against Braintree because someone wasn't playing well. During my first shift, I hit the ice and could not feel my legs. They felt like Jell-O because of the adrenaline pumping through me. The puck was in our end, and I raced after it. A Braintree player beat me to the puck and cut towards the middle of the ice. I absolutely tattooed him, and laid him out on his ass. We recovered the puck, and I hightailed it down to the other end of the ice. As we entered their zone, I got the puck on my backhand and shot a high hard one towards the net. It just missed the top corner and flew over the net. Had I scored, it would have gone down in high school hockey history as the greatest first shift ever.

The next day at practice, Coach Clifford had me take off my teal practice jersey, which had identified me as being on the fifth line and sentenced to mostly scout team stuff. He had me switch with a kid on the third line with me taking ownership of his blue jersey. It was a dream come true. I had officially been rewarded with a spot on the third line just in time to take the ice against our nemesis, Walpole.

It was a tradition to have a pasta dinner before the Walpole game, when the team would give each other the crazy bleach-blond haircuts. My buddy Brendan cut my hair and gave me a one-of-kind original: a half Mohawk that left all my curly hair flowing down my back. The next day, we all met at Tyler Gover's house for oranges and Gatorade before making our way to the high school to board the bus. The bus ride was completely quiet for the entire trip to Walpole. During the fifteen-minute trip, no one said a single word. We were focused on the mission ahead, each thinking our own mantra and getting internally pumped up for the game. Once we took the left-hand turn into the parking lot, the bus erupted noisily. We were screaming at the top of our lungs and were clearly fired up to play. The transition from silence to chaos was indescribable, and I could feel the blood pulsating in my neck. We were ready.

We got to the rink early and warmed up in the tunnel. We peeked out of the tunnel into the stands, in much the same way that a young dancer peeks through the curtains to size up the audience before a show. We could see the place already filling up and reported to one another that it was going to be a crazy night. As we were getting dressed, we could hear the crowd grow to capacity. I was so nervous. Ryan Donaghy cracked a joke, but I could not even laugh. I was focused but, honestly, shitting my hockey shorts. This was the biggest game I had ever played, and I needed to reach deep inside to gather my composure. We all preparing to head out when Coach Clifford charged into the locker room to fire us up. "The fans are hanging from the rafters out there," he screamed. After his pep talk, we bolted out of the locker room and onto the ice; somehow, I was the second one out after the goalie. I stepped onto the ice with my back to the crowd. My head rattled as I skated over to the bench; it sounded like the roof was going to blow off the arena. I threw my extra stick onto the bench and turned to peek over my shoulder. The stands were standing room only and the crowd two or three people deep. It was the highlight of my short-lived high school career.

We ran three lines throughout that game, and I recorded an assist on the first goal of the game. This would end up being my only point scored as a varsity player. In retrospect, it makes me feel a bit like Archibald "Moonlight" Graham in the movie *Field of Dreams*, who finally made it to the big leagues but never had the opportunity to bat. Though I, at least, had an opportunity to take a swing, my varsity hockey career would end up being nearly as brief as Graham's. My career varsity line score would end up as 0–1–1.

Nevertheless, we dominated the game start to finish that day and beat Walpole by a score of 6–3. Our feet never touched the ground from the moment we left the ice to the second we exited the locker room. The bus ride home was the complete opposite of the trip there with everyone standing up, screaming out the windows, hugging, and celebrating the entire way. We arrived at the high school, and there were carloads of people waiting for us and rejoicing at the victory we had brought back to Norwood. Students banged on the side of the bus as we pulled into the parking lot. Though this was no Stanley Cup celebration, sipping from the cup of victory never tasted so sweet. It is a moment and a game I will never forget.

We were scheduled to play Natick at home on the following Wednesday before the now-infamous game against Weymouth on Saturday. Because our fans were out of control at the Walpole game, they were banned from coming to the Natick game, so there was no one in the stands at all, and it was a bit eerie playing in an empty arena. The game was the absolute antithesis of the Walpole game, when the arena was packed to the rafters, and the emptiness of this arena actually helped put things in perspective. We won the game against Natick, meaning we rode a two-game winning streak as we prepared for Weymouth, when the fans would be allowed to return to the stands. Obviously, they were then unaware that they would be there to witness my date with destiny and unaware of how my life and theirs was about to be impacted.

Though I had no concept of how long I was down on the ice, I awoke from my temporary visit to La-La Land and tried to gather my composure. Though foggy from my head-first crash into the unforgiving boards, my mind snapped back to the seconds before I was hit, replaying the event like a tic-tac-toe pass shown on the Jumbo Tron above the ice at the TD Garden (also known as Boston Garden or The Garden). At the very instant that I looked to my skates to gather in the wobbling puck, I was bumped from behind by a Weymouth player, Tyler Piacentini. With both hands grasping my stick and my head facing down, I searched for the puck, hoping to regain control before taking it the length of the rink for the game-tying goal. But I lost my balance slightly as Tyler bumped me.

The first thing to hit the immovable boards was the top of my helmet. Had I remained in control of the puck, my head would have been up, as it should have been, and I'm sure I would have been able to brace myself with my arms before hitting the end board. Instead, the crown of my head went into the boards, and I slumped to the ice like a rag doll.

In actuality, Tyler was simply attempting to make a clean hockey play as we jockeyed for the puck. Hockey is a game of individual battles, and the team that fights to win each confrontation is likely to ultimately end up with the winning score. Tyler and I were both playing the game hard, trying to outmuscle the other in order to gain possession of the puck. A split-second the other way, and I would've been the one behind him. There was no malicious intent, and to this day that sits better with me mentally. Had the hit been brutal or had a roughing penalty been called, I may not be as comfortable with the way my life was instantly impacted. The fact that I was injured playing the game the way it should be played leaves me with nothing remotely resembling anger or regret.

As I came to, my first instinct was to get back in the play. That's one of the primary things you are taught: after you get hit, you get up, shake it off, and get back into the play. There may be no tougher individuals in all of sports than hockey players, and that is due to the mindset that you are never truly hurt until the play is over. Every Bruins fan remembers the 2013 Stanley Cup playoffs when Gregory "Soupy" Campbell played for nearly a minute with a broken leg after taking a slap shot to the shin while attempting to kill off a penalty. I tried to get up onto my skates, but nothing happened. I tried again and nothing. It was if my brain was having an altercation with my body, ordering it to get up and chase the damn puck, but my limbs resisted. I started to hyperventilate and panic before blacking out again.

When I head-butted the boards, I crumpled to the ice on my side. My body faced the net, helmet twisted, my stick now strewn a few feet away. My right cheek, resting on the ice, began to freeze on the cold surface as the arena *oohed* in unison before suddenly going silent. The crowd waited in hushed anticipation, hoping I'd get back up on my feet, shake off the pain, and skate back to the bench. When it was clear that simply wasn't going to happen, the collective silence of the entire crowd was ominously painful.

I lay in a heap only a few feet away from my parents, who were watching the game together from behind the glass. This was very unusual because they rarely watched my games side by side. Dad always hung with the rest of the fathers near one corner, shooting the shit with the guys, while the ensemble of Hockey Moms stood in a different area of the rink and did the women's version of the same. The moms were no less knowledgeable of the rules and ways of the game and, in fact, may actually have been a bit more passionate in shouting out their sentiments with every rush up the ice or at any play they deemed to be borderline illegal. The dads, on the other hand, were focused and silent, only increasing their volume on occasion when a play appeared to be misjudged by the referee or the linesmen.

I opened my eyes a brief time later and found myself face-to-face with Mrs. Cathcart. She is the mother of Brendan, my longtime teammate and one of my best friends. By day, Mrs. Cathcart works as a nurse, so she instinctively rushed onto the ice through one of the doors at the end of the rink when the referee saw I was seriously hurt and stopped play. She was down on the ice calmly trying to loosen my helmet and chinstrap as I less-than-calmly gasped for air.

Mrs. Cathcart was in my face, urging me to relax as I began to panic about being unable to inspire my legs to move. She instructed me to breathe slowly. Her words were firm, yet calm, and I tried to compose myself. I turned my head slightly, trying to gain focus, and noticed that my mom was also on the ice. I looked at the bottom of her jeans, noticing that they were wet above her ankle. This came with the realization that she had been on the ice for a while. It was then I knew I was in trouble.

Fortunately, I wasn't experiencing any serious discomfort whatsoever, which at first seemed encouraging. I assumed that if something was broken, I would be in an immense amount of pain. Instead, my body was engulfed by a complete sensation of numbness. As I tried to send another message to my legs, it felt like there were hundreds of pounds of wet concrete blanketing me. I called Mrs. Cathcart closer and told her I needed to say something to Mom, who stood a few feet away with a worried look on her face. Mom came to me and leaned over to hear my words.

"Mom, this is serious," I said. "I can't move, Mom. I can't feel anything. This is serious." I repeated the same sentences four or five times. In retrospect, I probably shouldn't have said anything at all because the words pierced right through her. Up to that point, I'm sure she knew this wasn't your run-of-the mill stinger, but hearing your son utter these words is something no mom ever wants to hear. Though trying to remain strong, the look of worry on her face turned to desperate concern. I can't imagine that any parent would know how they would respond upon seeing their child lie helplessly on the ice. Mom remained strong yet scared.

Meanwhile, a small group, including both of my parents, an EMT, and Coach Clifford had gathered around me. Though my thoughts were focused solely on comforting my parents at the time, I remember how eerily silent the entire rink was. Whereas minutes before the student bodies from both teams cheered raucously with each breakout towards the opposing net, now the crowd was no longer an assembly of opponents. Everyone had become one contingent, joined in mutual silence, hoping, hugging, wishing, and praying for me to rise to my feet. If the love and concern that filled the rink at that moment had been capable of healing, I would have risen to my skates and made my way to the bench. Though graciously appreciated, even the overwhelming outpouring of support wouldn't be enough to create the 2010 version of *Miracle on Ice*.

Mrs. Cathcart asked if there was anything she could do for me as she wiped the perspiration that had built up under my nose. Lying in the fetal position, I told her I wanted to see Brendan. Coach Clifford barked at Brendan to "get over here." I can still hear the ice cracking beneath my head as he hopped the boards, skated over and got close to me. He got down on one knee with a look of concern that only a best friend can display. I uttered the same words to him. "This is serious, buddy. I can't move. I can't feel anything." We both started to cry as my best bud tried to console me. Mrs. Cathcart then said to him, as only she can say, "If you're not going to help, then get out of here." I'm sure if she wasn't surrounded by others, her command may have even contained a commonly used expletive. Brendan rose to his feet and skated to the bench to share the unsettling news with the rest of the team.

My teammate and close friend Austin Glaser tells me that, before realizing the severity of my injury, he thought that I was being a drama queen and was just lying on the ice to get attention. To this day, he still teases me about a game we played in junior high when he first encountered my flare for the dramatic: "You went down after getting hit in the nuts and just rolled around like you had gotten kicked by a mule. All the guys on the bench were laughing while you tugged at your groin in agony."

Austin acknowledged, however, that this time things were a bit more worrying than a hit to the testes. He later said, "I quickly realized it was serious after I saw no movement, but I did not want to believe it was as serious as it appeared."

In 1995, Boston University hockey player Travis Roy was permanently paralyzed, only eleven seconds into his first ever shift, when he careened head first into the boards. University of North Dakota player Mitch Vig stepped aside innocently to avoid his first check as a collegian, and Roy crashed just as I had done. Roy dropped motionless to the ice, where he lay face down until he was removed from the ice on a stretcher. The awkward hit caused the blond-haired phenom to crack his fourth and fifth vertebrae, rendering him a quadriplegic.

I had read Travis's book, *11 Seconds*, when I was in middle school. He talks about the collision with the boards and describes how, as he lay there, the ice around his mouth was turned perfectly smooth sheet of ice by his hot breath. I recall vividly reading those pages several years earlier and thinking how weird that was. As I remained on the ice, I glanced at the surface below and saw the area right around my mouth was a perfectly smooth sheet of ice. Unfortunately, that wouldn't be the last experience that Travis and I would share.

The ambulance finally arrived, and I was ever-so-carefully lifted onto the stretcher after my neck and back had been immobilized. I was wheeled off the ice towards the door at the same end of the arena. The crowd remained respectfully silent.

In any sporting event, when a player is wheeled off due to injury, you see the injured athlete acknowledge the concerned crowd. Every fan has witnessed the familiar scene of a raised finger, a fist, or a hand in the air to reassure the crowd that everything is going to be okay. The fan base sees the token gesture and breathes a collective sigh of relief. I tried to do this, actually planning my exit move in my head as I was being lifted onto the stretcher. I felt as though it was my obligation to quell the nerves of the fans; to reassure them that number three was going to return to skate again before the next game. I tried with every fiber of my being just to raise my hand to let them know I was okay. Nothing happened. A sense of frustration enveloped me and nearly brought me to tears. I wanted to show my gratitude as the crowd broke their long silence and gave me a standing ovation as I exited the rink. Reserved yet loud, and in unison, both schools' supporters applauded. Again, I tried desperately to send a message to my hands. Nothing. Everything felt so heavy. I was being suffocated by layers and layers of wet concrete. For the first time in my life my body wasn't working.

CHAPTER 3
A New Definition of Normal

Lying in the back of the ambulance, head immobilized and my body strapped to the gurney, I traveled toward the hospital. The ambulance ride was so slow. The driver had to take things extremely cautiously to avoid hitting any bumps that would rattle the ambulance, as my neck was not stabilized at that point. Any sudden movement could dislodge bone shrapnel, causing more damage than I already may have sustained. It's not unheard of for an injury of this kind to cause only temporary paralysis, so at this time, the goal was to keep everything still and hope for the best. Though I sensed that my outlook was not a positive one, I held out hope that this paralysis was temporary or, better yet, just a bad dream.

As we made our way towards South Shore Hospital, normally a drive of about ten minutes, the EMTs and paramedics were busy, concentrating on examining my legs. Meanwhile, however, up at the other end of the gurney, I had begun to throw up. I had an oxygen mask over my mouth and nose, so the vomit had nowhere to go. It began to spew out of my mouth and out of the side of the mask. I did not want to aspirate and got their attention. They helped me clear my mouth and nose and got me cleaned up.

We finally arrived at the hospital and were able to pull up to the emergency room doors. An eye-popping blast of cold air, courtesy of the mid-winter night, came at me as the ambulance doors opened and I was gingerly unloaded. This drop in temperature was immediately offset by the sudden and welcoming warmth of the emergency room as I was wheeled inside the bright hospital. I was met by a full staff of nurses, physicians, and specialists, who were all scurrying around the emergency room with a sense of purpose and clearly wasting no time.

One of the doctors grabbed a pair of shears and deftly cut off my jersey and then my chest protector. I still have the jersey to this day as an eerie memento of the event. A friend of the family later stitched it back up, and it hangs proudly on my bedroom wall. In a rather masochistic way, I wish I had seen it all cut up as a reminder of what I had gone through, but I'm thrilled to still have it in my possession.

I was hooked up to an IV and immediately had a medicine cocktail flowing into my veins. The meds brought on an instant feeling of calm, and I became more comfortable as they began to take effect. A beautiful nurse appeared next to me, as if out of fairy tale, and took my blood pressure. For a moment I honestly thought I was dreaming. She had dark hair, dark eyes, and perfect facial features. She was a beautiful Italian-looking girl, probably in her mid-twenties. Though committed to Meghan, I looked at her affectionately as I began to flirt. As a fifteen-year-old, filled with raging hormones, it seemed the only thing to do at the time. After all, as a varsity hockey player playing the injury card, I honestly believed I had a chance. I told her she was really pretty. She smiled at me as I proceeded to throw up onto my chin and down onto my neck. "Probably not the best first impression," I said. Both she and the rest of the emergency room laughed. *So, you're telling me there's a chance*, I thought to myself, quoting one of my favorite lines from the movie *Dumb and Dumber*. Even while in pain, with my future hanging perilously in the balance, my sense of humor was sharp.

Likely out of a sense of guilt after my failed attempt to score me a nurse, my thoughts switched back to Meghan. *Someone needs to let her know that I might be late tonight*, I thought. *Our first official date has encountered a slight road block.* I chuckled inside, thinking of all kinds of excuses people come up with. "The dog ate my homework" or "I overslept" were nothing compared to the mother lode of all excuses. Never in history has a woman heard, "I'm sorry, honey. I'm going to be late for our date tonight because I'm paralyzed from the neck down." That thought, as funny as it may have seemed at the moment, snapped me back to reality. I thought, *Man, this is going to be difficult. If I am paralyzed, this is a real game changer.* This was my initial realization that life as we knew it may have officially changed. *This isn't a stint on the disabled list,* I thought, *or even a lost season. This may be my equivalent to Travis Roy's eleven seconds.*

When Meghan heard about the injury via an endless barrage of texts from multiple sources, she didn't know whether or not to take it seriously. After numerous texts, which boldly stated "Matt broke his neck," our mutual friend Mark called her. Apparently, his voice was shaking as he broke the news to Meghan that I was paralyzed.

"My heart sank, but I got off the phone and believed that you were going to be fine," Meghan later shared with me. "Give it two weeks and he'll be the same old Matt." That was Meghan's optimistic attitude, until she found out that I was being moved to Atlanta. It was then that she came to the realization that my injury was quite a bit more serious than she had first hoped and believed.

I zoned out for a bit while lying on the table, and my thoughts were focused entirely on Meghan. I daydreamed about how our friendship had gradually blossomed into romance over the past several years. This led up to what was to be our first official date that night, had things not unfolded as they had.

I can't exactly recall the first time I met Meghan. She attended Balch Elementary School in Norwood, and I went across town at Prescott. I believe I first noticed her at the youth soccer field or hanging around one of the Little League fields. Not that Meghan wasn't memorable, even in middle school, but I actually got to know her father better than I got to know her.

Mr. O'Connor, Meghan's dad, went to high school with both of my parents and played football with my dad. The summer before I went into high school, I would often see him at the baseball field watching the high school and American Legion teams play. Many of the fathers stood just beyond the outfield fence around their cars, talking about the game while enjoying a few libations. As my friends and I would cut through the gate to get to the field, he would often yell over to me "Hey, Matt. You better stay away from Meghan!" I would quickly joke back, "Too late, Mr. O'Connor. I'm seeing her tonight!" He would jokingly raise a fist and take a false step towards me as I took off with my friends, laughing; not yet fully cognizant of what the future had in store.

When I was in middle school, girls were not overly high on the hierarchy of my interests, so my courtship of Meghan was really nothing more than playful banter with her dad. A few years later, after I grew a bit of armpit hair and my voice changed, I found that my interests also changed.

Freshman year started, and by either a stroke of divine intervention or fate, Meghan and I shared an occasional class together. During daily study halls, we began going to the library together, doing our homework, and hanging out. October rolled around, and my level of interest began to intensify. I'm not sure if it was her incredible beauty or her really great sense of humor that attracted me first, but I couldn't help but feel that she was a complete package. Her appearance on the outside was complemented by her incredible beauty on the inside. She was genuine and always looked for the good in everyone and everything. I'm not sure if time really stands still whenever I'm alone with her. It certainly feels like it does. Each second that passes, each random thought we share, each spontaneous gesture we experience together seems like it is freeze-framed in my mind forever. She was also an athlete, which checked another box for me. Perhaps her most endearing quality though was that she didn't take shit from anyone.

Thoughts of Meghan vanished when the doctor came over and asked me how I was feeling, startling me out of my fantasy. The answer was "not good." My body was starting to shut down, and my breathing was becoming labored. The decision was made that I needed to be intubated. A tube was about to be put down my throat so that I could breathe with the help of a machine. Again I thought, *This is serious.* Having a tube jammed down your gullet makes it a whole lot different than a visit to the ER for a broken ankle or a dislocated shoulder. It is some serious stuff when they are preparing to help you breathe in the event that your body can't do it on its own. I've never claimed to be a Rhodes Scholar, but even I had come to the conclusion that this wasn't your ordinary boo-boo.

My mother filled me in on the details regarding what was going to happen. She leaned over, kissed me on the forehead, and assured me that everything was going to be okay. Both Mom and Dad were strong and holding it together, as they did throughout, but Mom was the true rock. I've developed an inordinate amount of respect for both my parents and will never be able to repay them for the sacrifices that they have made to care for me. Like a parent who does not have a favorite child, I do not have a favorite parent. I love them both in their own special way, but Mom exhibited strength and resilience that cannot be imagined. Whenever I even considered throwing in the towel or crying "no mas," Mom would remind me that giving up was not an option and I'd snap back to reality. They say that God gives nobody more than they can handle, but I'm not really certain that is true. An injury of this magnitude is truly a test to determine the mettle that a family is made of. From the moment I was injured to this very second that I'm writing this book, my family has exhibited strength, determination, and belief that somehow, some way, everything was going to be okay. Never have they wavered. At no point have my mom, my dad, or my sister Kelley allowed me to get too low or spend too much time feeling sorry for myself. Don't get me wrong. Some days are better than others, but whenever I began to question things, my family has always been there to remind me just how lucky I am.

The staff prepared me to go in for an MRI and a CAT scan so that they could determine how much damage I had actually sustained.

When the results were in, it was clear I needed to get to a hospital that was more equipped than South Shore to care for an injury of that magnitude. I heard conversations between staff that they were preparing to transfer me to the Boston Children's Hospital.

As Mom kissed me on the head again, I told her that I loved her and drifted off to sleep. Amazingly, I woke up four days later at Boston Children's.

Recently, I met a woman from Norwood who was in the emergency room that night. The woman told me that the entire ER staff were in tears upon witnessing Mom kissing me and me mustering up the strength to reciprocate just as I dozed off. I still didn't get a kiss from that cute Italian nurse I had puked on, but at that moment, Mom would do just fine.

While heavily sedated by very powerful drugs during my four-day hiatus from the world, I experienced many weird hallucinations and several extremely vivid dreams. I can proudly say that I have never participated in any recreational or non-recreational drug-taking, and if those visions were any indication of what the experience is like, I will gladly stay away from getting high indefinitely. We've all had some pretty crazy dreams in our lives, dreams like going to math class with no pants on or having a tea party with a raccoon. But the dreams I experienced in hospital were like something out of a 1970s Timothy Leary LSD experiment.

During one nightmare, I imagined that I was on the second floor porch of a triple-decker house in the heart of Boston. I stood and peered over the railing, looking out over the entire city while wearing my hospital gown. My view of the city was suddenly interrupted by a red syrupy liquid that began to drip from the third-floor porch overhead. I looked up and was met with a vision I will never forget. There was a man, also dressed in a hospital gown, removing 180 staples from his own leg. One by one he was pulling them from his skin as the blood dripped down. His screams pierced right through me, and I vividly remember the volume of his hair-raising yelps.

I couldn't escape the dream, despite trying desperately to wake myself up. The higher he got on his leg removing the stitches, the more the blood covered me. I tried to move away, but of course, my body did nothing. Blood got closer and closer to my face. I'm sure someone who performs dream interpretation would be able to explain in detail what this nightmare meant, but for me it was absolutely petrifying and still haunts me to this day.

I was also freaked out by a dream that I describe as a Cirque du Soleil show involving a naked woman in my hospital room. Now, to a fifteen-year-old, anything with naked women would usually be a welcome dream. This dream, however, was the complete opposite, and it haunted me nearly as much as the stitch-pulling and blood-dripping. The women would crawl across my ceiling and swing through my room, attacking and tormenting me. They made fun of me while knocking over the machines in my room. It was an absolute night terror. I could probably interpret this one a bit more easily, but again, I'll leave that to the experts.

During my first few days at Boston Children's, doctors performed my first surgery. This would be the first of seven surgeries I would undergo over the next seven years and the most serious of them all. It had been determined through the MRIs and CAT scans that I had broken my C4 and C5 vertebrae the moment I hit my head against the boards. These were the same two that Travis Roy had injured. I underwent surgery to put steel rods in the back of my neck and a cage in the front of my neck to help stabilize it.

I was slowly removed from extreme sedation, so my initial memories of the days that followed the surgery are extremely blurry. The horrible dreams subsided, and I was eventually restored to my new definition of normal. Normal is a really difficult word to define because what I knew as "normal" only yesterday had forever changed. Prior to my injury, normal was the only thing I knew and what I expected to experience throughout my life. As a teenager "normal" included getting up early, bounding down the stairs, grabbing a quick breakfast before I whisked off to school or an early morning practice, and annoying teachers and disrupting my classroom throughout the day. I'd spend some time with Meghan, punch some friends in the arm, wolf down some cafeteria food, and annoy some more teachers. From this day on, I'd still likely find a way to annoy teachers and disrupt class, but everything else included in my definition of normal was sure to be redefined.

Though every injury is slightly different, the doctors explained to my family and me that damage to the spinal cord that relates to the C4 vertebra, directly affects the diaphragm. Most times, patients with damage to the C4 require a ventilator to assist with breathing, have a very limited range of motion, experience paralysis in the arms, hands, torso, and legs and have trouble controlling their bladder and bowel function. He then explained that damage to the spinal cord at the C5 vertebra affects the vocal cords, biceps, and deltoid muscles in the upper arms. Unlike some of the higher cervical injuries, however, a patient with C5 spinal cord injury will likely be able to breathe and speak on their own. That was comforting for me to learn. Losing my ability to use my arms and legs was difficult to accept, but being without my ability to speak or breathe on my own would be nearly unbearable.

Though increasingly alert, I woke with the tube still down my throat to assist with my breathing and a tube in my nose to give me nutrients. There is not much else that will make you more aware that your life has changed drastically than waking from a long, deep sleep with a tube shoved down your throat. Eyes open, you look around a strange room with unknown doctors and nurses bustling in and out, and suddenly you realize that you have a piece of plastic tubing shoved inside you.

I was poked and prodded everywhere at all times of the day and night without warning. I was essentially being kept alive by the machines around me while my body acclimated to its new normal. The adjustment was not only a physical one but a mental and emotional one as well. My body had to teach itself how to breathe, to ingest and digest, while my mind and my emotions needed to learn to do one major thing: accept.

I woke and asked Mom all kinds of questions. The type of questions one would expect while learning to make sense of the fact that life can change in an instant. One day I am a young, vibrant, energetic teenager thinking of things like hockey, girls, hockey, hockey, and girls; then, in a moment, without warning, I'm thinking about my own mortality and spending my life sitting in a chair and having tubes protruding from nearly every orifice of my body. I am not sure I am able to convey how precious life is and how you should take advantage of every opportunity to appreciate the small things. The realization hit me hard: the realization that I'll never again experience the feeling of sand between my toes or grass under my feet, or that I can be hugged but no longer have the ability to wrap my arms around a loved one to reciprocate, or that a fly can walk across my forehead to taunt and torture me but I don't have the ability to swat him off my face.

Life can change dramatically in an instant.

In the moment I was sitting there with Mom, I struggled mightily to make sense of any of it. *Why me? What did I do to deserve this? Why? Why? Why?* Mom sat on the edge of my bed running her hands gently through my hair. She tried to calm me down and let me know that everything was going to be okay. Though I appreciated her strength, reassurance, and sense of calm, "okay" was not what I wanted to hear. I wanted to hear that I'd get better. I wanted to hear that they were going to cure this thing right away. I wanted to know that with the best medical attention and advances in science I'd be able to step right back into life with nothing more than a few scars and a really incredible story to tell.

I was frustrated and confused. I couldn't talk very well with the tube going down my throat, but Mom knew what I was getting at. She knew I wanted answers. Of course she knew; she is my mother. Mom assured me that, at some point, we'd sit down and try to figure out logical yet honest answers to the "why" and the "why me." But for today, we just needed to concern ourselves with rest and relaxation. Mom was right, of course. We'd have plenty of time over the coming weeks and months and, unfortunately, years to try to answer those seemingly unanswerable questions. We weren't going to uncover the secrets of the universe from my hospital bed at Boston Children's, but in due time we would find the opportunity to try and sort things out.

CHAPTER 4

The Boys Are Back in Town

Though my mom and dad remained outwardly strong, on the inside they were as torn apart as I was. Their lives had changed as drastically as mine. They were sentenced to the unenviable chore of caring for me while also trying to keep the Brown family ship afloat. Internally, their world was thrown into a state of chaos; externally, their hands never shook and their faith never wavered.

Mom's sense of calm was evident on one of the first nights following my arrival at Boston Children's. She walked into the room after taking a brief break from my bedside and found a nurse caringly brushing my teeth. The memory is forever etched in her mind because it was such a dramatic thing to witness. She stood and watched without saying a word, extremely careful not to interrupt this very powerful moment. The event was not staged and obviously not rehearsed, yet it was a clear signal that the curtain was not about to drop on the Matt Brown show: if the incredible staff at Boston Children's was taking the time to care for my teeth, there was obviously a belief that I would need to use them again. She saw it as the first visible sign that everything was going to be okay, and she talks about it to this day.

Dad was there also, offering me a healthy dose of support, and he stayed in my room with me for hours on end as well. Dad was more emotional than Mom, however, especially during the early days following the injury. In our family, like many, Dad wears the captain's hat, but Mom is actually steering the ship. Mom went right into game-plan mode. What do we have to do now and how do we have to do it? She was in charge of the game plan and played the role of coach, captain, and quarterback. Dad was there to comfort me and to tell me that everything was going to be okay. Not to any way diminish the role that Dad played, but he took on the position of the cheerleader and the backup quarterback. Both of them played invaluable roles, and my recovery would have been badly impacted had I been missing either one from my team.

There was a bench with cushions next to the bed in my hospital room. My parents would take turns trying to get comfortable on it and would stay with me throughout the night. One would stay one night while the other would go home and try to get some real sleep. The next night they would swap. I can't say that they accomplished a whole lot of sleep while keeping me company each night, but my whole family made sure that I knew I wasn't going to go through any of this alone.

Kelley was also at the hospital every day. She was a first year high school student, and I'm sure this threw her for a loop. Her days were suddenly filled with unexpected attention and an endless barrage of questions about how I was doing. I'm sure she was happy that everyone was so concerned about me and our family, but freshman year is a year to focus on yourself and your life, and having so much attention directed towards me was not anything she signed up for. Despite that, she was the president of the unofficial Matt Brown fan club, and she kept my morale high even during my darkest, most difficult days. She always found the humor in everything, similar to the way her big brother would approach life situations. She also acted as a social liaison, keeping me in the know about what was going on at school and how the town was reacting following my injury.

The town of Norwood responded in full force and wasted no time adopting me as their honorary son. About a week or two after I was hurt, my mom was asked to visit the high school to speak on the morning announcements. The school was concerned about my well-being, and Mom was tasked with providing them with an update. As she entered Norwood High she was absolutely awestruck by the outpouring of love and affection that she witnessed from the moment the front doors of the school opened.

She was approached by Brian Lopez, who used to drive me to school every morning. He reached into his pockets and presented a stack of cash earned from sale of T-shirts that he had created. Everyone had the number three emblazoned on their shirts and painted on their faces. Throughout the town, number three hung in people's front doors and on yard signs. Threes were in storefronts and windows of buildings throughout the downtown area. Someone had spray-painted the number three on their windows as a show of support. Rumor has it that a cop stopped by because this was reported as an act of vandalism, but he soon realized it was actually a show of support and not malicious at all. The notes, letters, get-well cards, pictures, and poster boards that flooded my room at Boston Children's were enough to have erased the USPS deficit. Every day, I received hundreds of gestures of encouragement from friends, family, and perfect strangers, again reminding me that I was not going to go through this alone and that the community had my back. This provided me with the strength and commitment to do everything in my power to recover as quickly and as thoroughly as I possibly could. Though I was very early in my healing process, I was beginning to view this as an opportunity, not a tragedy. I was beginning to see the injury in a more positive light and occasionally began answering the question of "Why me?" with the response "Why *not* me?"

Not only did my wonderful hometown of Norwood respond in full force, but people from all over the state, the country, and even the world heard about the paralyzed kid from Norwood and sent me tokens of their love and support. I received a note from the Greek national hockey team sending their *agápe* (love). Then jerseys started to roll in from many of the people in the hockey community that I have long idolized. The first jersey I received was from Boston Bruins forward Patrice Bergeron, one of the most highly respected players in the NHL. The jersey came with a signature and a handwritten note on the back: "To Matt—stay positive!" I also got a personally signed jersey from The Great One, Wayne Gretzky. Jack Parker, the longtime head coach of the Boston University Terriers hockey team visited me, along with his team captains, while Jerry York of Boston College came in with his captains and the Beanpot. (Now, I grew up a Terriers fan and would go see the tournament every year, so though I was thrilled to see the actual Beanpot in person, it would have been so much more exciting if it were in the hands of Coach Parker and BU!) Former Bruins captain, Number 77 Ray Bourque, came in to see me. I could not believe the size of his chest. I swear it must have been a half an acre. Ray used to play thirty-five minutes a night, which is unheard of. He was an absolute stud. I was also visited by Kenny Casey and Scruffy Wallace of the world-renowned Boston band the Dropkick Murphys. Their huge hit "Shipping Up to Boston" is synonymous with this incredible city and has become a huge part of Boston sports lore. They also happen to be huge Bruins fans and hang with many of the players. There really was a revolving door through which the legends of hockey past, present, and even future visited me on a daily basis.

It's never escaped me that being injured in such a public manner has afforded me some perks that most people do not get to enjoy. If there's such a thing as a sexy way to become paralyzed, having it happen while playing the game you love in front of hundreds of fans and a compassionate media would be it. I can't imagine that people injured while driving or falling down a flight of stairs, or even those born with disabilities, receive the same level of support that I have been blessed to receive. For every Matt Brown who is injured in front of a crowd of supporters and taken under the wings of the townspeople, sports legends, and entertainment notables, there are thousands of people who lie alone in their hospital room or apartment and don't receive a fraction of the attention that I've been lucky enough to receive. I'm in no way trying to glamorize what happened to me, and I wouldn't think twice about trading my current life in exchange for the life I once knew, but I fully understand that my plight has allowed me to experience things I never would have known had I cleanly picked up the puck and avoided injury. I lay in my bed many nights and counted my blessings that despite a major dose of bad fortune on that fateful January night in 2010, I'm still one of the lucky ones.

The head nurse while I was at Boston Children's was a guy named Dennis Doherty. Dennis grew to become not only my nurse but also my friend, my savior, and my guardian angel. My three weeks at the hospital would have been impossible without him. He made me laugh constantly and became as important to my healing as any medicine that was ingested or injected into my body. He knew when it was time for people to come and visit, and he recognized equally when it was time for people to leave me the hell alone. He knew when I needed my rest and when I needed to have my spirits lifted. This guy was instrumental in my physical recovery, my emotional well-being, and my mental health. Dennis and his family live in Norwood, and I occasionally see him around town still. Whenever I have been to Boston Children's following my injury, I make sure I stop at Section Seven South, which was the intensive care unit during my stay. I see Dennis and the rest of the staff who took such remarkable care of me. Dennis was a lifesaver and I am forever grateful for the care he provided.

Like a blast of unexpected sunshine, the entire Norwood team came to visit along with some of their parents. The parents all chipped in to rent a coach bus so that the team could travel to Boston as a unit to visit. Because the mothers knew it was going to be a rather emotional and powerful day, they purchased everyone on the team funny glasses and an assortment of gadgets to lighten the mood and keep everyone loose. As the players exited the bus, they were nervous and unsure about what to expect upon seeing their fallen comrade for the first time. No one wanted to be left behind, and in their haste to enter the hospital, and a serious case of "boys being boys," they ended up jamming the revolving door, with all twenty-five of them mashed into the same section. To make it more ridiculous, the team was attired in their blue jumpsuits that, as one of the parents commented, made them look like Smurfs.

When they were finally shoe-horned out of the revolving door, they made it upstairs and came in to see me in groups of five or six at a time, so as not to flood my room. My parents spoke with the group briefly beforehand, so they knew what to expect and weren't alarmed by all of the machines that I was hooked up to. The parents hung outside in the waiting room. It was just like old times … with a few minor alterations. Dennis was right outside the door, and he had his eye on me through the window, making sure everything was okay. It could have been a bit overwhelming, and though I certainly handled it, Dennis always had my best interest in mind. It's part of what made him as incredible as he was.

The seniors came in first, then the juniors, then some of the coaches. The last group to come in was my core group, comprising the under classmen. Their visit was exactly what I needed. It was so wonderful to see the guys, yet extremely emotionally challenging at the same time. We laughed a bit and shed quite a few tears. Seeing a group of teenage boys sobbing is not a sight you see every day, but it is indicative of what a close-knit group we all were. Some of us have been friends since we were toddlers and had played hockey together since the first day we laced up skates. Over the previous two months especially, I had been with the entire group every day. We were together at school, on the bus to practice, and on the bus home. We were a unit at games and during team pasta dinners. We were like an army platoon, together 24/7, always knowing what the other was going to say or think and always having the other guys' backs. The fact that one of the soldiers had taken a fall was, I'm sure, rather unsettling.

They looked around the room at all the swag I'd accumulated and marveled at the signed Bergeron jersey and the sweater from Gretzky. I'm sure that not one of them wanted to swap positions with me, but there were several comments about how lucky I was. Skate a mile in another man's skates and they may not feel the same, but I do understand what they were getting at.

It was really difficult for me to speak, since I was still intubated, so everyone tried their hardest to understand the words that I was attempting to mutter. It's sort of like that new game called "Watch Ya Mouth" where players shove a plastic mouth piece into their lips and try to utter phrases like "bell bottoms and blueberries" while others try to guess what was said. My speech was nearly unintelligible, so I spent most of the time listening. I just sat, looked at them, and nodded on occasion trying to take it all in. It was just what I needed at the time, and I believe it was sort of what the team needed as well. Sometimes the unknown is a bit scary, and seeing me, though battered and bruised, comforted them. I watched them all walk out, and as the door closed behind them, the waterworks started. I wanted to leave with them and go back to the normal times we had. Instead, we'd all have to accept that "new definition of normal" I wrote of earlier.

I've said all along that I'm lucky. I didn't sustain a traumatic brain injury that would have altered who I am. My body may be broken, but inside I'm still Matt. This was comforting to them. Once they saw me and spent even just a bit of time with me, they left with a sense of reassurance. Sure, they knew that number three may not be taking the ice with them any time soon, if ever, but at some point, at least, he'd be able to cheer them on from the stands.

As I lay in bed, I thought a lot about Tyler. I wanted to make sure he was okay. Yes, I was the one who was physically injured, but I couldn't imagine the sense of remorse that he must have been feeling. As I said earlier, there was nothing he did that was malicious, and even though that was more comforting for me, I am not sure that the same could be said for Tyler. I didn't know him any more than I knew any of the other guys on the Weymouth squad, but I was quite sure he was a nice guy, who was likely hurting due to the consequences of his very innocent actions. I wanted to know what was going through his mind and to share my concern for his well-being. I asked my mom frequently if she thought he was okay. I told her that I wanted to see him, and she said absolutely not. She was not angry at him, she just didn't think it was wise for him to see me with all the wires and tubes coming out of me and surrounded by all types of medical machines. I completely agreed with her decision once she explained it to me. It just wasn't the right time, and it would not be fair for him to see me in my current condition. At some point, I knew we would connect, and hopefully when I was further along the road to recovery.

There was a prayer service held at St. Catherine's Church in Norwood during the week after I got hurt. At 6:00 a.m. one day, St. Catherine's opened its doors to the townspeople of Norwood. Kelley and my dad were among the attendees to visit the church. They weren't expecting many people and were surprised that the entire church was packed, while a line of people waited outside in the cold for their turn to say their prayers. Tyler, his family, and several of his teammates made the trip up from Weymouth before school and hugged both my sister and my dad. This was a class act by a first class kid, and I'm sure a few tears were shed by everyone who witnessed the meeting. My dad assured both Tyler and his teammates that everything was going to be okay.

CHAPTER 5

Sealed with a Kiss

Seeing the boys enter my hospital room as a unit brought my mind straight back to the game against Weymouth. I'm not sure if I had taken the time to think about the actual game a whole lot since the injury happened. I've played the injury itself over in my mind thousands of times, to the point that it is still the only thing I ever think about. I have developed a one-track mind and spend every waking hour thinking about the moment I hit the boards. I never thought about the game itself nor a whole lot of anything else. I began to ponder how difficult it must have been for the guys to continue playing periods two and three after seeing me carted off the ice. And how challenging it must have been to take a hit or lay into an opposing player without tensing up just a bit. I wondered if they had rallied behind me, all revved up and ready to win one for the Gipper or if they had collectively peed down their legs upon having to continue the battle without one of their soldiers. Either response would have been acceptable. I try to put myself in their skates, but I'm not entirely sure how I would have responded. If it were a fairy tale or a Hollywood movie, I know how the script would have played out, but reality tends to be a wee bit different than fantasy. Somewhat to my disappointment, the game continued and Weymouth dismantled us by a final score of 5–2. I'll give my guys a free pass for this one, since they likely had something else on their minds. The final score wasn't very important. The lives of everyone involved, whether a player or spectator, had probably been forever altered.

The following Wednesday after the Weymouth game, the team had played at Milton. During the first period of the game, one of my teammates, Chris O'Brien, was checked into the boards, and oddly enough suffered a head injury also. Once again, the crowd held their collective breath and, I'm sure, feared the worst. After an ultra-cautious twenty minutes on the ice with the medical staff, Chris was taken off on a stretcher and ultimately diagnosed with concussion. He was taken to Boston Children's for observation and came in to see me while I was still sedated. I'm sure he did a bit of thinking at the hospital about how lucky he was. Like any sport, hockey is a game of inches, and whereas I was unfortunate enough to careen into the boards with my head held in a "perfect" position to sustain paralysis, Chris was fortunate enough to escape with a mere bump on the melon.

My sister Kelley, who was at the Milton game, texted my mom as Chris was down on the ice: "Mom, Chris O'Brien just hit the boards and is lying on the ice." My mom thought she was joking and told her that she wasn't being funny. My sister convinced her it was true, and an understandable lump formed in my mother's throat. After Chris was wheeled from the ice, with the ability to utilize the thumbs-up gesture that I had failed to use, the coaches, referees, and administration made the very sound decision to cancel the rest of the game as a precaution. Many of the players were a bit wigged out about the eerie coincidence that they had just been forced to relive. Thank God Chris was not as badly injured as I was. I'm not sure the team, the school, the town, or even the sport of high school hockey would recover from two catastrophic accidents in as many games.

Following my injury and before the game against Milton, there was actually serious consideration of forgoing the rest of the season. The team discussed it as a unit and made, in my mind, the correct decision to continue. They knew that's what I would have wanted had the proverbial skate been on the other foot, and it was the right decision to press on. No war is called off when one soldier is shot. Any squad needs to use a tragedy as a rallying cry and find it within themselves to continue. It would have been bullshit had they canceled the season because of me.

Immediately following my injury, some of my teammates harbored a bit of a vendetta against Tyler. It is human nature to be angry when you see one of your teammates go down, and in a case of historical revisionism, they remembered the hit as dirtier than it really was. Without the luxury of replay, some of the team decided that Tyler could have avoided the hit if he had really wanted to. Some kids at school started posting on social media that we needed to retaliate next time the two teams met. A few of the parents, the coaches, and some of the more level-headed guys on the team yanked the pitchforks away from the lynch mobs, and cooler heads prevailed. It was decided, instead, that we needed to show some class and support the Weymouth side instead, and when Weymouth next played at Walpole, a group from Norwood showed up in their blue sweatshirts to support Weymouth. The guys stood and cheered for them in the stands and when they came off the ice: a gesture that makes me proud to be from Norwood. It was the proper way to handle things, and it left both squads with a feeling of closeness instead of hatred and anger. Once again, life is ten percent what happens to you and ninety percent how you respond to it, an adage that rings true in my life more so now than ever.

News travels fast in a small town, and Meghan caught wind that the team had come to Boston Children's to visit me. Her first reactions were anger and a bit of jealousy that the boys were able to spend time with her man before she had. She wanted to be the first to see me, and though that was understandable, I was extremely happy to see both the team and my girl, Meghan. She came in a day or two after the boys, about eight days after the accident. When I saw her walk through the doors my heart melted all over again. I know we were just a couple of teenagers, but what Meghan and I seemed to have was really more than puppy love. We had a very special relationship, and every moment we spent together was memorable. Seeing her walk into my room caused me to drift back and think about how our budding relationship had ultimately evolved from a friendship to a mutual crush to so much more.

Entering Norwood High as a sophomore had felt totally different than the same scenario one year earlier. As a freshman, you're really still a boy, viewing this whole new world with wide-eyed innocence without a clue as to what you are about to embark upon. You are naïve about the likelihood of being made fun of, you are the lowest on the totem pole—the rookie, the plebe. As a sophomore, on the other hand, you're still in the bottom half of the high school caste system, but at least you have a year's worth of experience under your belt. You know the lay of the land around school, have an idea as to what to expect, and feel more confident when walking through the halls.

Being a part of the hockey team made the sophomore experience even better. This was one of the driving forces that whet my appetite for making the varsity grade so badly. I wanted to be riding on the varsity bus to games and to be a part of the varsity group in the hallways. High-fiving a junior or senior varsity teammate is way better than being stuffed into a locker by one of them, like the JV's often are. Not only did the guys take notice, but the girls did too … and aren't they all a high school boy thinks about?

During the fall of sophomore year, I was talking to a girl named Jess. We had gotten close over the summer, and our closeness carried into the start of the school year. Like many teenage boys, I was a bit fickle, and my head was on a swivel whenever a member of the opposite sex walked by. I soon realized that my interest in Jess was fleeting, and my feelings switched to Meghan. When I saw her, I got butterflies, and I felt like I needed to be perfect around her. I tried to be on my game and look good all the time. I wanted her to see the best of me, even though that was only a façade that I would not be able to sustain forever. Meghan enjoyed hanging out and talking with me, too, but I have no idea if she considered me anything more than her friend. I always say that if I could have one superpower, it would be to have the ability to know what girls are thinking. That way,

I would know if she had the same feelings as I did and, therefore, if I even had a shot. I've later learned that knowing what women are thinking is a superpower that every man would love to have and would likely pay a small fortune to purchase.

During our study periods, a group of us would go to the library under the pretense of "getting some work done." It was there that our friendship began to flourish. Our conversations continued from class to class and carried on throughout the entire day. It didn't take long for me to realize just how cool she really was.

Around the middle of November, my hockey tryouts and her basketball tryouts were about to start. We began to talk all the time, both inside and outside of school. We texted regularly about classes and school gossip, but spent a majority of time talking about tryouts and our respective sports. She had played for the JV team our freshman year, so her heart was set on making varsity as a sophomore. I had the same goal. Tryouts for both of us took place the week after Thanksgiving. Each day after tryouts, we checked in with one another to see how things had gone. At the end of the week, we both shared the disappointing news that neither of us had made varsity.

As odd as it seems, that shared disappointment was actually a blessing of sorts because we provided support for one another as we both dealt with the realization we hadn't made the grade. We'd exchange stats after games and pushed each other to "keep at it" to prove to both our coaches that they had made bad decisions in not selecting us for the big squad.

Around this time, I began to realize I had feelings for her. Our once-innocent conversations now contained a fair share of flirtation. I even mustered up the nerve to float a trial balloon out there by mentioning my interest to one of her friends, who encouraged me to follow my feelings. Instant messaging was huge at the time and we would stay up late chatting on AIM (AOL's instant messaging app) before swapping over to Skype, where we could not only chat but also see each other. It wasn't exactly the same as being together, but it was the next best thing. Some nights we even virtually fell asleep on each other as we Skyped so late we crashed in between conversations.

On New Year's Eve, the guys and girls got together at Mary Kate Galvin's house. I was fairly confident that Meghan and I had the hots for each other at this point and were both planning to use the midnight clock strike to our mutual advantage. Everyone had a great night, culminating just before midnight as couples gathered around the TV listening to the sounds of Ryan Seacrest counting down from sixty.

Meghan and I had spent much of the evening sitting up against the wall laughing, talking, and flirting a bit more than usual. As I heard the group begin counting down from ten, I looked at her and our eyes met. A nervous smile came across both our faces as I went in for the kill. Our lips met and everything around us in the basement seemed to go quiet. I don't know how much time passed before we came up for air, but we could both feel the eyes of most of the party guests homing in on our locked lips. A round of gentle laughter ensued when we finally parted lips, and both Meghan and I turned a matching shade of red.

In the weeks to come, our relationship began to flourish. Meghan wore my away jersey in the stands at my home game after I got called up, and she wore my home jersey at away games. She came to all my games, and we spent most of our free time hanging out together, alone. I made the decision to take our relationship to the next level and ask her to go steady. I wanted it to be clear to the world that Meghan was mine and I hers. I wanted to be the one who called her "my girlfriend."

I mapped out everything the night before I planned to ask her to go steady to ensure that everything would go smoothly. On that Friday, we had a half day of school because of midterms. Students were released at 11:30 a.m., and the team had a practice scheduled for 2:30 p.m. Meghan's mom picked us up after school let out and dropped her daughter and me at my house. It was the first time I had met Mrs. O'Connor. Unfortunately, I still had the bleach-blond mohawk from the Walpole game, which both Meghan and Mrs. O'Connor absolutely despised.

After the obligatory stop at my refrigerator to grab an after-school snack, we sat on the couch. It was my time to "propose." My throat was dry and my palms started to sweat as I mustered up the courage to tell her what was on my mind. I told her I wanted to take our relationship to the next level. I wanted to make it official and make her my girlfriend. My stomach tightened, and I could feel my heart beating through the material of my Norwood High T-shirt as I waited for Meghan to respond. I sat there staring at her uncomfortably for what seemed like forever but, in truth, was about three-quarters of a second. A smile came over her face and she said, "Yes. Absolutely yes."

Though so much had changed since that unforgettable proposal, seeing her walk into my hospital room was exactly the medicine I needed. I was head over heels for her and remained so for several years after the unexpected cancellation of our first official date. Before my accident, I would see her every single day in nearly every one of my classes, so eight days without seeing her felt like an eternity. I could not erase the smile from my face as she entered the room. Her reaction was guarded but pretty much the same. When she first walked in, it was intimidating; I sensed that she hadn't realized the magnitude of what had happened to me until she saw me with her own eyes. Much like the guys seeing me for the first time (probably even more so), Meghan needed to brace herself for seeing me with wires and tubes protruding from my body. The boy that Princess Leia had fallen for now looked more like C3PO than Luke Skywalker.

Even though seeing her was out of this world, not being able to reach out and hug her was very difficult for me to accept. I asked her about school and what was going on there. We talked for a few minutes about what people were saying and how the school had been so supportive. She said, "Enough about that. Let's talk about us." This made me feel so much more secure knowing that there was still an "us" in spite of everything that had transpired in the last week.

Despite my limited ability to communicate with the tube still inserted into my throat, we spent the next several minutes chatting about the everyday stuff that we would have talked about anyhow. We were so happy to see each other that the severity of the injury was honestly never discussed. We didn't talk about our future, although she knew it was going to be a long road and a far different future than either of us had fantasized about. We were just so happy to see each other that it didn't matter at the time.

When we ran out of things to say, we sat there awhile, just the two of us. For that period of time, though way too short, everything felt perfect. It was so appreciated that Dennis and our parents left us alone to talk. As much as I loved her parents and mine, it wasn't them I really wanted to see.

When it was time for her to go, she leaned in, gave me a kiss and left. I have to admit, I was not in an ideal kissing situation. I had machines surrounding me, and the railings on my bed were pulled up. I had a tube going into my nose and mouth. Just to add to the challenge, the tube going into my mouth had tape all around it. Nevertheless, Meghan made her way between the wires and the tubes and navigated her lips to the side of my mouth. She wasn't really able to lay one on me, but the kiss was perfect nonetheless. So very perfect. It was exactly what I needed to carry me through until the next time we were together. It also, for the first time in over a week, allowed me to think of something other than hitting the boards. For the next eight days or thereabouts, the only thing I thought of was Meghan and the kiss.

Seconds after Meghan left the room. I sat for a moment with an ear to ear smile (or as close as one can have to that with a tube taped to their mouth) thinking about the girl I loved. My brief moment of reflection was broken, when her mom came back into the room with a bag in her hand. She reached into the bag and pulled out a framed photo of Meghan. In the picture, Meghan was wearing a dark-blue sweater and a huge smile. Meghan was too embarrassed to give it to me, but I absolutely loved it. It went right onto my nightstand while

I was at Boston Children's and then made the journey with me when I was transferred to Atlanta. Each night, therefore, for the next several months, Meghan was by my side as I dozed off to sleep and helped to give me the inspiration to dedicate myself to the hard work that would be necessary to make it home again. And when I did go home at last, it was next to my bed there, too. I found myself looking at it when times were tough and when my mind would wonder to places that I didn't want to go. Even when thousands of miles away, the image of Meghan provided the essential ingredient in the recovery recipe: hope.

She actually came to see me again, a couple weeks later, on Valentine's Day. In anticipation of her visit, I had my cousin, Alex, run down to the CVS in the lobby to buy her a box of chocolates and flowers. She was extremely surprised upon receiving them and even accused me of sneaking out of my bed against doctor's orders. If only I had the ability to do that! Meghan kept the flowers on her nightstand until they were beyond dead as a memory and token of our love for each other.

Communication was quite difficult while I was intubated. There were times when I needed a drink of water, a scratch, or the channel changed, and it's difficult to imagine how ordinary tasks become second nature until those abilities are suddenly stripped from you and you have to ask for help. It becomes necessary to adjust in order to perform tasks that were simple only a short time before. Scratching, combing, brushing, wiping, and even talking all required assistance and a dose of ingenuity. In order to communicate, we devised a board that contained four groups of five letters and one group of six: letters A through E made up the first group, then F through J, and so on. Whenever I had something to say, Mom or Dad or Dennis would point to a group, and if the letter was in that group I nodded. They would then try to home in on the correct letter in the group. We would continue our primitive guessing game until they figured out the word or phrase I was hoping to convey. The discovery of the letter board was extremely important, as I could finally communicate without gagging on my tube. One morning, while Dad was sitting next to my bed, I got his attention by clicking my mouth to indicate that I had something to spell. The click was a slight press of the tongue to the roof of my mouth similar to the clicks used in some African languages. Dad responded to my click and came over with the board as I was sort of scrunching up my nose. I was hoping he would get the hint without having to spell, but was sadly mistaken. We started going through the board, and I spelled I, followed by T, then C, then H, then Y. Itchy. *My nose is itchy, Dad. Scratch it. Pretty simple*, I thought. However, Dad interpreted it as two words: IT and that ever-popular word CHY (long I sound). He kept repeating it in that manner. IT-CHY. IT-CHY? I continued to play charades scrunching up my nose, while Dad kept repeating IT-CHY. My eyes started to well up with tears as I became increasingly frustrated. I just wanted to scream at him "SCRATCH MY F'N NOSE, DAD." He finally figured it out, but by then, of course, my nose was no longer itchy or even IT-CHY for that matter. It's a funny anecdote today, but at that point it was a clear reminder of how very helpless I had become.

It was hard to imagine that just a week or so earlier, I was scratching my own nose, brushing my own teeth, getting myself a glass of water, and accepting a kiss from Meghan without even thinking about it. Now, my Dad had to scratch my nose (eventually), a nurse brushed my teeth, I breathed through a tube, and my girlfriend had to limbo under tubes to give me a kiss. This was just a glimpse into what life was going to be like moving forward.

Soon after, thankfully, I had the tube removed from my throat, and I had a tracheostomy. A hole was made in the front of my neck into the windpipe, and a breathing tube (a "trach") was then placed through the hole to help me breathe. It wasn't until I arrived in Atlanta that the ventilator was hooked up to the trach, so I still couldn't talk very well initially because the trach didn't allow air to flow over my vocal cords. The trach was like a balloon that goes around my windpipe, so though there was air flowing through the vent, it was difficult to make sound. I was able to mouth the words, however, and the ability to combine that with the spelling board, made communication quite a bit faster. Once I arrived in Atlanta, they deflated the balloon so that I could talk.

Also, when I was intubated, I wasn't allowed to drink anything. There were times when I would wake up and my mouth would be as dry as the Sahara. It was likely because of the meds I had to take, but I swore I'd exhale out dust at times. I would beg the nurses to shoot just ten milliliters of water into my mouth. They would comply but use the tiniest syringe and shoot only enough into my mouth to wet my palate. I was so grateful. But when the tube finally came out, I was happy to enjoy one of life's simple pleasures; a drink of water. I was also able to nibble a bit of food.

I would be remiss if I didn't mention once again how important Dennis was to me at this stage of my recovery. Things were changing for me nearly every day. Adjusting to a new way of life was more of a mental change at this point than a physical change. The physical adjustments would commence once I began therapy, but at this point the goal was to begin the mental adjustment of accepting life as a paralyzed individual. It was so huge to have someone like Dennis taking care of me and being in charge. He was with me all the time, setting everything up and making sure I had the best nurses on my schedule. He gave me my meds, he made sure I was comfortable, and he rolled me from one side to the other to prevent bed sores. Most importantly, he talked to me. We would joke around, and his mere presence made things brighter. In many ways, he reminded me of Robin Williams's character in the movie *Patch Adams*, without the red nose. In actuality, all of the nurses did a wonderful job. I can't stress enough how very thankful I am for nurses. I made a point of making that apparent when I spoke at the Worcester State University Nursing Program graduation ceremony. "Nurses," I said, "are more than just people who check vitals and dispense medication. They are hand-holders and tear-wipers, conversationalists, clergy, mental health advisors, and most importantly they are friends. The doctors may make you well, but the nurses allow you to heal."

CHAPTER 6

Recovery through the Eyes of the ICU Nurse

By Dennis Doherty

As a nurse, your role is to provide holistic care not only for the patients but also for their families. Being a good nurse is more than simply changing dressings and bedpans, but more about healing the patient and their family—inside and out. I met Matt on the Monday morning following his injury, about thirty-six hours after his arrival at Boston Children's. The round-the-clock media onslaught had only just begun, so upon arrival at my shift, I hadn't yet heard about Matt or his injury.

Caring for someone with a new spinal cord injury is extremely challenging; there is so much that is unknown in the early stages following the injury. The most difficult piece is trying to help the family navigate the whole situation. I have faced some very taxing nursing situations during my career, but the first half of that shift was among the most demanding. The third shift nurse gave me a thorough report during the transition between our shifts and told me the story of what had happened. I immediately felt sick to my stomach. I questioned how life can be so cruel when a typical high school kid, playing a sport that he apparently loves, can experience such a traumatizing and potentially life-altering event. My oldest son was just a year old at that point and, as a new father, reading the report hit me hard. But when I learned that Matt was from Norwood, where I had moved to the fall before, it really hit home. Feeling the connection increased my desire to provide the absolute best care possible. I always give everyone a high level of attention, but learning that the town of Norwood would be watching me and rooting for Matt's recovery filled me with a heightened sense of responsibility.

I entered Matt's room and introduced myself as a fellow Norwood resident. The family gave me a curious look as if to say, "No you're not because we know everyone in Norwood, and we do not know you." I told them that I grew up in Dorchester, but considered myself an honorary Norwood native since moving there a few months earlier. The town's support of Matt and the Brown family was interesting to experience, because on the way to and from work I would witness "3" or "MB3" displayed by businesses and on automobiles, front lawns, and fire trucks. It was exciting to know that my family had opted to move to an amazing town that was thoughtful enough to rally around one kid. I assured my wife that we picked the right community to call our home. I'd then go to work to participate in the drama that was actually playing out on the front pages of the *Norwood Record*.

After meeting the Browns, my nurse mode kicked in. Upon acknowledging your own internal feelings and emotions, it's time to suck it up and get to work. During the first couple of days, my role was to support Matt with excellent nursing care, keep him comfortable, and to constantly assess his neurological, respiratory, and cardiovascular functions. These three assessments are extremely challenging because he was medicated and intubated, and because there was concern about the shock that his body just took.

While doing that, I needed to check in with the family as well. They are in shock also and trying to comprehend what has just occurred. They are attempting to process not only what happened to their loved one but also how their lives are about to be impacted as a result of it. As a nurse, I approach this situation with the family by simply being present. There is no textbook that says "do this" or "do that," so I trust my gut and bear witness to the whole thing. There are a lot of providers constantly coming in to assess the patient and update the family regarding the patient's well-being. A family in shock is not processing any of it at that stage, so I keep track of the plan, translate it for the family, prepare them for what to expect, and help them make sense of who is who, and who is responsible for what.

After the first few days, nursing care broadens. Primarily, you push the patient to participate in their own care, while engaging the family in the patient's care as well. Something as simple as giving a bath becomes a big deal. It is a task that they haven't done or even considered doing since the patient was a child. Now they find themselves thrust back into the role of caregiver and have to suddenly reestablish themselves in that unfamiliar role. Facilitating the family in helping with activities like that is a starting point.

In Matt's case, he had a tracheostomy and was on a ventilator for respiratory support, so encouraging the family to participate in some aspects of that care is more challenging. I gave Mr. Brown the package of suction catheters saying, "Just hold it and play around with it." I wanted him to simply get comfortable with touching, holding, feeling the equipment at that point. At the end of the day, the family is going to have to learn how to care for their patient. Parents and caregivers in this situation are suddenly being asked to become critical care nurses, so we must teach them how to work a ventilator, suction out the airway, and troubleshoot things. It is a lot for them to process and to comprehend. When a family is with me in the ICU, my role is to set a realistic picture of what is coming and empower them to begin providing care for the patient. A lot of the independence for both the patient and family happens after the ICU, but it starts from a pretty early point with the ICU nurses.

I learned very early on that Matt is a remarkable young man. As a patient, he inspired not only me but also the rest of the nurses who cared for him, because he really attacked the whole thing head on (literally). I never heard him say anything negative. Once he had his surgery to stabilize everything, he was focused on rehab and on what he needed to do to experience a full recovery. There he was in a bed in an intensive care unit, hooked up to all this technology, and his attitude was, "Okay, let's get to work." He is extremely funny and constantly cracked jokes with everyone. He even busted my chops! But he made my job easy.

Being a sports fan, I really enjoy hockey and believe it is the most athletic of all sports. Up until a couple of years ago, I could not ice skate, so my admiration is huge for someone who can not only skate but also whistle a puck down the ice while keeping their balance. When my oldest son got into hockey, I learned to skate, so I now really appreciate the athleticism on display. I went to Northeastern University, so my wife (whom I met there) and my friends from school follow the men's hockey team pretty closely. I also follow the Bruins. All that aside, my love for hockey grew even more after seeing the support that the hockey community offered to Matt. Within a few days, his entire ICU bed space was filled with signs, cards, autographed jerseys, and memorabilia from players. It was incredibly impressive.

Matt had a ton of visitors, maybe the most of any patient I've ever taken care of. As a result, we needed someone to manage the visitors. The Browns know a lot of people. It seemed as though the whole town of Norwood was trying to visit! Then all of these hockey players began coming in. I was not caring for Matt when the Bruins players came, but I was there for a few notable visitors, namely Travis Roy. Charlie Coyle was another big-deal player who came in to see Matt as well.

When the entire Norwood hockey team visited, it was a logistical challenge. We have an unofficial guideline of two people at the bedside at a time, so accommodating an entire hockey team is a nightmare. There is likely a policy somewhere stating that we would not support an entire hockey team visit, but in this instance we made it work. I created a waiting area for them downstairs near the cafeteria. Matt's Aunt Nancy took on the job of escorting players up seven floors to the ICU. They would come in four or five at a time and then switch out. I felt for the kids. I could see that a few of them had a tough time seeing Matt in his current condition, but the kids tried to keep it light so as to ease any level of discomfort. One kid made Matt a card that made fun of the condition of the Norwood Country Club's fairways, since Matt was a golfer in addition to playing hockey. The visit was important for Matt, for the Browns, and for the team as well.

One evening, near the end of shift, the desk called to say there was yet another visitor for Matt. I told them that I would send out Matt's mom, Sue, because Matt's day had been packed, and I really wanted him to get some rest. Sue came back into the room and said, "It is Coach Jack Parker and some players from the Terriers." I was like, "Fine, but make it quick." I laughed because as a Northeastern grad and hockey fan, BU is the enemy. I was disappointed in myself for turning my back on my alma mater, but I caved in for the emotional uplift that it would provide to Matt. I did consider dropping the gloves with the Terriers on their way out, however.

The visit that stands out the most to me was an appearance from Dan Cummings. Dan had suffered a spinal cord injury several years earlier and then started the nonprofit called Journey Forward, which is dedicated to bettering the lives of those with spinal cord injuries or disability. He walked in using a walker and talked with Matt. I was in his room because I was setting up meds and witnessed how very emotional their visit was. I heard him encourage Matt saying, "You're not going to give up. You're going to do this. You're going to walk." It was clearly an inspiring visit for Matt, but it was for me as well; witnessing a conversation like that helped make me a better nurse.

One would think that media coverage doesn't have an impact on nursing care, but it did create a lot of traffic in terms of visitors. People mean well, and they want to help and be supportive, but caring for a critically ill patient is difficult as it is without a constant flow of visitors. The support for Matt and his family was incredible. I have never witnessed anything like it, but as the nurse, you have to balance the attention with what is best for the patient. In the last half of his admission, Matt was really working hard with physical therapy and was drained. Rest and recovery are important, especially in a critical care setting, so I had to conserve Matt's strength during this very important period. There was so much support in the form of visits that the nurse has to play the bad cop at times—not just for Matt's sake but his family's. It is important for Matt, Michael, Sue, and Kelley to know that they are not alone, but there were times that I sensed they were exhausted from talking and telling the story over and over again or attempting to provide the many updates that caring friends requested. We formed the type of relationship, however, where I could comfortably advocate for Matt to rest and for the Browns to have a break without upsetting their visitors. I believe they appreciated that.

I have the utmost respect for the Browns. Seeing the support network they had was incredible. They know a lot of people, and *they* handled the injury and the recovery similarly to how Matt attacked it: they remained light, very positive, and extremely funny. This approach went miles in helping Matt recover as well as he has. Michael cracked jokes, and that is when I knew the entire family would be all right.

Now, several years since having Matt as a patient, I love seeing the young man he has grown into. He remains the positive, funny, hardworking kid I met in the intensive care unit. He has obviously had to mature quickly as a result of his accident, and also as a result of what he has grown to mean to the community. I am excited to see what the future holds for him.

I have a friend who is a cross-country coach in Weymouth, and I am the nurse at the preseason cross-country running camp that he operates. After my first year working there, I encouraged him to bring Matt to the camp to speak to his team. Matt had more than 250 high school athletes, counselors, and coaches completely engaged as he shared his message of "don't take anything for granted, surround yourself with good people, and when you face adversity, attack it head on." Hearing him speak to this huge group made it apparent how much work Matt has put in since I met him. He is now in a position where he can have a positive impact on the lives of others.

Generally, when you care for someone, you are unlikely to know how your care ultimately influences their recovery. On those occasions when former patients stop by the unit for an appointment, for example, you experience one of the greatest joys as a nurse. Their return reinforces why we all followed the calling of nursing. You are constantly evolving as a nurse. Each patient, each family encounter, and each new experience helps you grow professionally. Matt certainly had an impact on me. In the ideal patient/family-nurse relationship there is a synergy that is palpable. But while you attempt to provide excellent care for all patients and families, understanding and embracing what is unique about you as a nurse is important. I think that working with Matt helped me see that I bring something unique to nursing, specifically when caring for adolescent patients or working with their parents. Matt and I formed a bond that has empowered me to be myself at the bedside of an adolescent patient who might need humor and tough love, rather than another approach. The relationship I forged with Matt's father, Mike, was also unique. It opened my eyes to what I have to offer fathers of critically ill patients especially. I can point to other families where the father appreciated my presence, and I understand that it is because I bring a perspective that's different from the majority of my colleagues. I feel I have Michael Brown to thank for this.

For the last several years, I have transitioned to a professional development role in the nursing industry, so I do a lot of nurse education. I try to instill the idea of embracing your uniqueness whenever I can. Nurses are not all built the same, and there will be instances when you thrive and others when you will not. Understanding their own strengths and weaknesses will help each nurse grow professionally and help both patient and family flourish as well. Caring for a patient like Matt taught me lessons I may have not otherwise learned, lessons I try to teach to my current patients. The impact of having Matt as a patient will likely influence the care provided by nurses everywhere for years to come.

CHAPTER 7

The Fraternity of Hockey

As I shared earlier, the hockey community really came together to support me as one of their own. If you think about it, these guys didn't know me from Adam. I had unrealistic hockey aspirations and was not of the caliber that I'd ever play professionally or even Division 1—I was just a kid who loved the sport and had likely climbed about as high as I was ever going to ascend. Yet these guys, who only share with me a mutual love of hockey, came out in droves to support me as if I was a son, a brother, a teammate. Each day another legend or near legend would enter my room and make me feel that my collection of hockey cards had come alive and they became a part of my relatively insignificant life. At times it made me wonder if I were still hallucinating from being over medicated. Unable to pinch myself to prove their existence, I had to go with my gut and believe it was all real.

Past players who haven't stepped on the ice in years still let me know that they once played hockey and that they were thinking of me. The Greek national team sent me a message and best wishes in my recovery. NHL teams and players sent me jerseys and words of encouragement. College and local high school teams were doing the same. Fraternity is the perfect word for it. If one of us goes down, we do whatever it takes to lift them back up.

I am forever grateful to all of these members of the hockey fraternity who took time out of their busy schedules to visit me and support me and to assure me that they had my back. I'd like to think that if the roles were reversed and I were a star of the sport that I'd do the same. Thinking about it that way, I know I would. As a long-time participant in the sport, we've all experienced many of the same things: early morning skates, late night practices, long bus rides to games, gut-wrenching practices, the thrill of winning a close one and the heartache of losing the same. Having experienced similar things growing up in the sport, you develop a bond and a comradery with anyone who plays the sport, and in that feeling of closeness I understand how when a brother hurts, you hurt as well. It's similar to seeing two motorcycle riders who have likely never met, giving a gesture of acknowledgment when passing one another headed in opposite directions. They are brothers in spirit and wish each other well, despite neither one truly knowing anything about the road the other will be traveling.

During my stay at Boston Children's, Boston Bruins' longtime captain Ray Bourque came in to visit along with former Bruins defenseman Gord Kluzak. Seeing both of them walk into my room was mind blowing. Kluzak was the former number-one pick of the Bruins in 1982 and had his career cut short after only 299 games due to chronic knee issues. He underwent eleven surgeries. In many ways, Kluzak may have felt some of the same feelings as I did having been torn away from the game we both love due to injury. Kluzak's injury did not occur quite as suddenly as mine did, but that in no way indicates that the pain wasn't equally excruciating and the loss just as devastating. Since his retirement, Kluzak has worked for the New England Sports Network (NESN) doing the Bruins pregame. My future aspirations, once I proceed further down the road to recovery, are very much the same, and I hope to use my degree in communications to broadcast some portion of the game. During an away game, Gord (or Gordie, as he's known) mentioned that he had visited me and gave me a shout out over the air. It is extremely healing to be lying in your hospital bed licking your wounds, to hear the voice of the team you've followed from the time you owned skates wishing you well. I would absolutely trade that feeling for just one more game on ice, but it is still pretty darn cool to hear your name mentioned by one of the legends of the sport.

Weymouth native and winger for the Minnesota Wild Charlie Coyle stopped in with his mom to visit me at Boston Children's as well. Though Charlie grew up in Weymouth, he didn't play for its high school team. He went to Thayer Academy in Braintree, MA, and played on a select team, South Shore Kings of the Eastern Junior Hockey League. During his senior year, which was my sophomore, he appeared on the cover of *ESPN RISE Magazine*, a publication which features high school athletes. *ESPN RISE* referred to Charlie as a "can't-miss prospect" and one of the nation's top high school players. When the article came out, we all read it and talked nonstop about him. He was good friends with Tyler, so when he visited me, it was like being in the presence of a budding star, despite the fact he was only a year or two older than me. He brought in a South Shore King's jersey that was signed by the entire team. He also let me know that Tyler and the entire town of Weymouth was cheering for me. I learned that, after his visit with me, he had relayed the message to Tyler that I was doing okay and was in good spirits. Since then, he has been to visit me at my house several times, and I often see him whenever he is back in Massachusetts. Coyle has blossomed in the NHL, scoring 81 goals and 133 assists in his six-year NHL career.

Anyone familiar with the sport knows what a special guy Patrice Bergeron is. Bergeron is a four-time winner of the Selke Trophy as the top defensive forward in the game and a one-time winner of the King Clancy Memorial Trophy, which is awarded to the player who best exemplifies leadership qualities on and off the ice and who has made a significant humanitarian contribution to his community. Nothing shows leadership more than a guy who takes time out of his busy schedule during the most hectic portion of the season to visit an injured member of his fraternity. Not only was his jersey the first one I received but it came with a handwritten note, too. That gesture showed my family that he genuinely cared; it wasn't a message that some PR person put together for him. It showed how special he is, and he continues to be a wonderful friend to me. After my transfer to the Shepherd Center in Atlanta, the Atlanta Thrashers were in their next-to-last season of existence prior to their defection to Winnipeg. The Bruins came to Atlanta for an away game and flew in the night before. I received a notification from the team that Patrice was on his way to the hospital to say hello, taking time out of his schedule the night before an away game to come by and hang out. He stayed for about an hour and brought a duffle bag filled with Bruins sweatshirts, Bruins DVDs, and even New England clam chowder and Boston beans. Patrice also brought the gold medal that he won just a few weeks earlier for Canada at the Olympics. He allowed me to hold it, which was the equivalent of holding the Stanley Cup (something that I also was lucky enough to do in 2013) or sleeping in the Lincoln bed. My hands began to sweat as Patrice placed this symbolic piece of gold into my undeserving hands.

We got to sit around and shoot the shit. It wasn't a sympathy visit or something he felt obliged to do; it was a wonderfully kind gesture and the start of a beautiful friendship. At that point I was star struck by him. I asked him a bunch of questions about what the guys were like, what it was like to play in the NHL, and who the funny guy on the team was. Over the years, since that night, our conversation has become much less superficial, and now we are two buddies talking about life both inside and outside of the rink.

The Bruins donated a luxury spectator's box for the Bruins and Thrashers game and allowed me to bring along several friends. Most of them had never seen hockey before. There was a kid about my age, Ty Nelson, who had never seen a game and didn't know that they could fight during the game. He went nuts each time two opponents dropped the gloves. Bruins President of Hockey Operations and member of the hall of fame Cam Neely stopped by the box to say hello. I'm not sure if I was more excited to meet Cam Neely the player and the hockey exec or Sea Bass, the character who spit on Harry's burger in the movie *Dumb and Dumber*. Really this is a no-brainer as Neely the hockey player was the very definition of a big, tough, physical hockey player who was also a skilled scorer, averaging nearly a point a game and two minutes a game in penalties over his hockey career. Coincidentally, Neely's career also came to an abrupt end. This was due to a thigh injury sustained after an illegal hit by notorious cheap-shot artist Ulf Samuelson.

One of my closest friends from the NHL fraternity is former Bruin defenseman, Andrew Ference. Andrew was a sixteen-year veteran of the NHL, playing for the Pittsburgh Penguins, the Calgary Flames, and the Bruins before retiring after several seasons as captain of the Edmonton Oilers. He was with the Bruins from 2006 through 2013 and was instrumental in their Stanley Cup victory against Vancouver in 2011. My favorite Ference hockey moment came when he flipped off the Canadians' fans at the Belle Centre in Montreal in the 2011 playoffs and pleaded "equipment malfunction" stating that his hockey glove got stuck with the middle finger up. He later confessed to malice, but you just have to love the creative excuse.

I was introduced to and became friendly with Andrew and his beautiful family following an introduction from mutual friend, Sgt. Lucas Carr. Lucas and his Army Ranger squad actually flew a flag over Afghanistan for me following my accident, and Lucas brought it to the house after returning to the states, accompanied by Andrew and his family. Andrew brought a bunch of hockey sticks, and his kids even put their painted handprints on my wall at home. Following his signing with Edmonton, we went to The Garden to watch a Bruins playoff game together after the Oilers were eliminated. Sitting next to him was really awkward because he had a look on his face that expressed his desire to be on the ice with his former teammates.

When the Bruins won the Cup in 2011, each player on the team was allowed to spend a day with the Cup and celebrate in whatever fashion they chose. Andrew, who made his home in the North End of Boston, rode his bike to Spaulding Rehab Center in Boston pulling the Cup in a wagon behind. He invited me and my family, Lucas, Boston Marathon legends Dick and Rick Hoyt, and my co-author Todd Civin to join him while he shared the Stanley Cup with patients at Spaulding. He also invited us to dinner that evening in the North End with Lord Stanley's Cup sitting at the head of the table and being treated as the guest of honor. Andrew Ference and I certainly have a special relationship. He thinks about me, and I think about him. His wife Krista is equally incredible, as are his beautiful daughters, Ava and Stella.

During my time at Boston Children's, there was a pasta dinner held at Tyler Gover's house, and the entire Norwood team enjoyed a carb-filled meal the night before a game. Though my mom and one other parent were tipped off in advance, there was a loud, firm knock on the door as the team was sitting down to break bread. Mrs. Gover answered the door and welcomed in a giant of a man. The 6'9" Bruins captain Zdeno Chara walked into the living room, ducking his head as he made his entrance through the doorway. The team was in such a state of shock that no one moved initially, as if they had seen a monster. Upon realizing who he was, they burst out in screams and celebration of disbelief. He stopped over to let the team know that he was thinking of us and that it was important for them to support me. He even brought a cake to the dinner and spent some time talking to the boys and taking pictures. He even signed the wall of the Gover's house because he asked him to. The boys couldn't stop talking about it after he left, and it really picked up their morale.

At some point when I was down in Atlanta, Tyler Piacentini came to Norwood to hang with a bunch of the boys and go out to breakfast; another gesture of kindness that makes me proud to be a member of the hockey fraternity. It was important to exhibit that there was no lingering feelings or bad blood between the two groups. They grew up and handled it very maturely.

I have been extremely lucky to form relationships with such an incredible group of men. There are no other athletes like hockey players. I'm not certain what it is, but they are truly unique and treat their hockey brethren like family. To become friends with so many of them is surreal. The fact that my injury occurred several years ago and many still refer to me as their friend is a testament to the type of people they are. This connection includes not only the players but also management, the front office personnel, and the "regular Joes" who work at The Garden. When I visit, they are genuinely concerned about my well-being and are quick to let me know that they're still rooting for me. It's through that type of *esprit de corps* that I stay motivated and inspired to bust ass. To this day, all over Norwood and throughout the state, people literally and figuratively pat me on the back and encourage me to keep striving to get better. With a team like that behind me, there's no way I can lose.

CHAPTER 8

Goodbye, Boston; Hello, Atlanta

My parents had done quite a bit of research regarding the best place for the next stage of my recovery after the ICU at Boston Children's Hospital. In consultation with my doctors, we all decided that the Shepherd Center in Atlanta was going to be the best place for my rehab. Shepherd Center is a private, 152-bed hospital devoted to the medical treatment, research, and rehabilitation of people with spinal cord injury and disease, acquired brain injury, multiple sclerosis, chronic pain, and other neuromuscular problems. Though we considered going to Spalding in Boston for my rehab, which in many ways would have been far easier on my family, we felt that Shepherd would give me the best opportunity to rehab thoroughly.

A few days before I was ready to leave for Atlanta, the Dolans and the Maggios came to visit. Mark, Kyle, and I got to hang out by ourselves for a while. Melissa (Mark's sister), Kristin (Kyle's sister), and their parents came too, but the bulk of the time was the three of us enjoying a low-key evening. No hospital pun intended, but it was just what the doctor ordered. With Mark sitting one side of my bed and Kyle on the other, we talked about Atlanta and what we thought it was going to be like. They told me they would be cheering me on and rooting for my recovery. When Melissa and Kristin came in, both leaned over and gave me a kiss on the cheek. It was like we were all hanging out again (only before, there were no kisses). It was extremely reassuring to know that everything was going to be normal once I returned home.

Though I knew that the Shepherd Center gave me the best opportunity to recover, I was still really nervous to be leaving my family, my friends, my support system, and most of all, Meghan. Much of what kept me going to this point was the reassurance that I was recovering in my own backyard. The comfort of knowing that a friend was likely to stop in and visit at any moment prevented me from getting too low or too bored. Knowing I was soon to find myself a thousand miles away from home for the next three months, anxiety started to engulf me. As I got closer to leaving my new comfort zone, I was nauseous and experiencing some shortness of breath. The nurses sensed my trepidation and helped me accept it as the best option for me. It was something I needed to do to challenge myself and to push myself towards a greater recovery. Dennis assured me that I was going to be in good hands. He told me to go down there and bust my ass.

The nurses had lined up to see me off and wish me well as I was wheeled out of Seven South down to the ambulance. It was extremely emotional for me because these wonderful men and women had basically kept me alive since my accident. They had become my friends, my family, and my support system. They helped me to heal both physically and emotionally. They fed me, gave me my meds, scratched my itch, and wiped my ass. I saw all of their faces as I made my way onto the elevator, and I realized they were emotional too. Just as they had made a lasting impression on me, I guess I, along with my family, had an impact on them as well.

I was loaded into the ambulance for the ride from Boston to Hanscom Air Force Base. It had snowed just two days before, and everything in the city was covered in salt. I looked back through the salt-caked windows of the ambulance as the city of Boston disappeared behind me. The route took me by TD Garden, which to me will always be known fondly as either Boston Garden or simply The Garden. This was completely fitting, as the Bruins management and players had been so supportive to me throughout the journey and continue to be to this day. A lump formed in my throat as the building shrank into the distance as we passed over the Zakim Bridge and into Somerville. Far off in the distance stood the Bunker Hill Monument. Tall and strong, the monument was erected to commemorate one of the first battles of the American Revolution as the upstart colonial militia men battled the British Redcoats in order to gain our country's independence. I too was ready to fight the most important battle of my life, and though perhaps not as high an historical significance in our country's history, my battle seemed pretty significant to me.

I said goodbye to the city, knowing full well that if I worked hard and was up to the challenge, my stay in Atlanta would likely be only a few months long. Though the ride up I-93 was short, there was time to think back to the early years of my life in Norwood.

We all have an age when our conscious memory begins. I'd say mine takes me back to age two or three, though the bulk of my recollections take place post-preschool. Growing up in Norwood, I loved being with my neighborhood friends. Our neighborhood was a hybrid community that combined the worlds of *The Little Rascals* and *Stand by Me* because we kids managed to get in a bit of trouble while learning some valuable life lessons along the trail. Like most kids who grew up without cell phones and the Xbox, we spent about thirteen hours a day playing outside, beginning our summer days at about 7:30 a.m. and not heading home until the street lights came on. We had an absolutely perfect neighborhood, filled with about a dozen kids my age. We'd spend every waking hour running around the neighborhood and in our cul-de-sac, riding bikes, playing whiffle ball, touch football, tag or street hockey. We were never without something to do.

Different from kids today, I'd walk to and from elementary school from the age of six on without my parents. Like so many young entrepreneurs, I'd earn some money to buy baseball cards by selling the finest lemonade in all of Norwood. As I grew into my early teens, I closed the stand and was able to earn some cash cutting lawns in the summer and shoveling driveways in the winter.

I was an average student who fell into the category of slightly underachieving; I didn't study very hard because it got in the way of playing and having fun. My grades in elementary school were satisfactory, dipping to C's and B's in middle school before bottoming out in high school. Though never in danger of failing, I was also never in much danger of accidently stumbling onto honor roll either. I was a bit of a class clown, and though I respected my teachers and they enjoyed having me in their class, I probably would have benefited by shutting my mouth and paying a bit more attention.

I just love getting people to laugh and making them happy. I tend to push the limits here and there, and that may have gotten me into trouble with some of the teachers, but it was never malicious. My mom likes to tell the story about my parent-teacher conference when I was in the seventh grade. She went to the school intent on finding out if the Norwood educators were ready to hang me. All of my teachers were set up in the same room to greet the visiting parents. We had a long-term substitute for our math class, who didn't really know my propensity for chatting. When it was her time to speak, she said, "He is not going to get by on his personality alone." My English teacher leaned over and interrupted her abruptly, "I'm going to stop right there. Have you not met him? He is going to do anything he wants to because of his personality." That really stood out to my mom, who appreciated the fact that the staff recognized that some comic talent is not a bad thing during the course of a long school day.

There were occasions when I may have taken it a bit too far and the teachers would take me into the hall. I would respect their wishes and tone it down. It was actually my playfulness that Meghan found to be an annoyance when I was trying to find out if she was interested in me or not. I'd ask all of her friends what she was saying about me, and she'd tell them that I was a bit too immature for her. However, as it turned out, I grew up rather quickly following the game against Weymouth on January 23.

In terms of sports, like ninety percent of American kids growing up in the early 2000s, I kicked a ball around for a couple years playing youth soccer. I wasn't very good at it, but I did enjoy playing until I got older. I also played Little League baseball and Babe Ruth until I was fifteen, and though I made some good plays and had some memorable at bats, I'd classify myself as a bit streaky. However, I'll long remember my first time on skates.

Many who witnessed my maiden step onto the rink compared me to a young Ray Bourque. Nope, that's BS. Not even close. I absolutely despised the ice. I must've been around three years old, and because I was just a year or so removed from crawling, I guess it should come as no surprise that I spent more time on my ass than on my feet. Rather than Bourque, I more closely resembled Bambi when he nearly knocked himself senseless the first time he stepped onto the frozen pond. I crawled off the ice, bruised, battered, and humbled, vowing that I would never do it again.

About two years later, Mom helped me fulfill my destiny and took me to the Ponkapoag Rink over in Canton to learn to skate. Ponkapoag actually became our home rink for the high school before it collapsed during the winter of 2015. With only one lesson under my belt and a stick in my hand, those first five or six strides were the best feeling I had ever experienced. I didn't want to get off the ice. I was older and stronger, and I fell in love with it right then and there.

I took my game to the pond soon after that, and the guys and I would spend every winter waiting for it to get cold enough to skate down at Froggy's, Norwood's most popular pond. As we got older, we would try to find other ponds that no one knew about, since the ice would get chopped up from heavy traffic at Froggy's. We would spend the entire winter, from 8:00 a.m. to 8:00 p.m. every Saturday and Sunday, and a few hours each day after school, with a thermos of hot chocolate, a bottle or two of water, and some snacks, and made enough memories to last a lifetime.

I also played a lot of golf from a very young age, and there are days that I miss golf more than hockey. I started getting really good at it right before I got hurt and was actually beating my dad on occasion that summer. It was our time together, and that is the reason I miss it so much now. As a kid, Dad and I would go to the range and whack balls for hours. When Dad would participate in golf tournaments, he would take me out, put a ball on the fairway, and let me take a hack. I would hit it, he would pick it up, and put it on the green. In time, I was teeing off and playing the ball from the first to the eighteenth hole with them.

During my freshman year of high school, I tried out for the golf team but missed the cut by just a few strokes. I spent the fall season as a ball boy for the varsity girls' soccer team instead. My friend Ty Gover's older sister was on the team, so he and I would run up and down the field chasing after balls and looking at pretty girls. It was a suitable substitute for getting cut from the golf team.

Despite dabbling in golf and baseball, from sixth grade on I ate, slept, and drank hockey. That was all I wanted to do. Whether on a pond, playing street hockey, shooting pucks in the driveway or just watching highlights on YouTube, hockey was my passion. When we were in elementary school, the Norwood high hockey team were like stars to us: we idolized them. My uncle was an assistant coach, and after games we would beg him to sneak us into the locker room to meet the team. They were only sixteen to eighteen years old, but they were stars to us. In particular, I worshipped Sean Arthur, a hard-hitting defenseman who had a wicked slap shot. Ryan Henry was one of the better goalies in the state at the time, while Tony Verrochi was a forward who could hit the back of the net. It's so funny how things eventually come full circle. During warm-ups, when we finally made it to high school, we saw the faces of young kids with their noses pressed against the glass idolizing us, as we had done years before.

My NHL idols were Mike Madono, Sidney Crosby, and Alexander Ovechkin. They were NHL superstars from the moment they entered the league. My Bruins favorites had not been elevated to superstar status, but wearing the eight-spoke "B" logo of the Bruins made them instant stars in my world. Every game, whether the team was winning or losing, the boys and I would order a couple pizzas, tune into NESN, and watch Joe Thornton, Glenn Murray, Byron Dafoe, Sergei Samsonov, and a young budding superstar by the name of Patrice Bergeron.

During my freshman year at Norwood, I played on the third line of the JV team. For some reason, and I don't know why, I just went through the motions. We weren't very good, and that may have had a hand in it, but I look back and wish I put in more effort and played harder. Entering tryouts my sophomore year, I was committed to giving it all I had. I felt very confident and ready to make the step up to the varsity.

As with any sport, the more I played the more confident I got and the more my game improved. I "saw" the ice very well and became a relatively skilled scorer. I knew where my ice mates were going to be, and I was rather deft at finding the blade of their stick with a pass. I started skating more, training, and working out regularly. Before tryouts for the high school squad, I skated for the Norwood midget team as I mentioned earlier. The midget season begin in September and continues until Thanksgiving. This was a perfect opportunity for me to train hard and to be ready for high school tryouts. We only had an average of eight to nine players each game, so I was skating about thirty of the thirty-six-minute game.

When varsity tryouts rolled around my sophomore year, I felt like I was ready. I made it to the second to last day of cuts before being relegated to the junior varsity squad. Upon seeing my name among the list of cuts, I was devastated. I came home and broke the disturbing news to my parents. I was on the verge of tears and told my mom I wanted to quit. She knew better and knew that quitting wasn't an option. She went along with me, let me blow off some steam, and told me she would support me. She told me to think long and hard about it but knew that I had already made a good decision.

With a slight chip on my shoulder and a desire to show Coach Clifford he had made a mistake, I went down to the JV and I lit it up. The net seemed huge to me, and I was determined to score every game—most games I succeeded. The JV coach took notice and let Coach Clifford know how I was doing. Coach Clifford was also there for many of the games, so he was able to scout my sudden scoring prowess firsthand …

The ambulance turned onto Hanscom, and I was suddenly snapped back to present day. A blast of cold air startled me as the doors opened and I was wheeled onto the tarmac. Al Bishop, owner of Boston Air Charter and a Norwood guy, arranged the flight for us and graciously covered all costs. With Al at the helm, the flight crew included my dad, a paramedic, and me. I was given a healthy dose of meds to fight off a bout of anxiety, and the flight went smoothly.

My mom and Kelley had flown commercial to Atlanta the same day that Dad and I had flown down with Al, and they actually beat us down there. They were at the Shepherd Center when I arrived. They got me settled in and visited throughout the rest of the day. The nurse came in about 8:00 p.m. and advised my family that it was time to leave. This was quite a shock to them, since they had camped out in my room since the night the accident occurred. They were quite nervous leaving their boy with strangers, but they knew I was in great hands.

Upon my arrival at the Shepherd Center I was really sick. The doctors felt that my body was in shock from the trip down. I wasn't regulating my body temperature, and my blood pressure was all over the place. I spent the first few days in a hospital room before transitioning to my new home on the rehab floor. I sat in a chair, wrapped in a blanket. I was extremely cold and dizzy, and though I knew I was being overly anxious, I sat wondering if I was going to survive. This was an eerie reminder that my body wasn't out of the woods yet. Dad and I reminded each other that it was still important to take things day by day.

A day or two later, still sick and wrapped in blankets, I made my way to the gym. It was my first time in a wheelchair, and I rolled in wrapped up in a blanket and feeling small. In my mind, I looked like E.T., the extra-terrestrial from Spielberg's movie, in the bicycle scene. I entered the gym and immediately realized that this wasn't your typical hospital physical therapy room, but a real gym. Everyone was on mats and working their asses off. Seeing people standing and using the electric stimulators was extremely inspiring, and the sight made me feel that as soon as I stabilized, I'd be on the road to recovery.

My floor was made up of kids mostly my age because it was the adolescent program. There were between twenty to twenty-four patients in my group. This made acclimating extremely easy because we could relate to one another. Had we been with patients who were older, we wouldn't have bonded as quickly. Being with others who were my age and had experienced a similar fate made things flow a lot better. We fed off each other and encouraged one another to work hard, though none of us knew for sure what our ultimate fate would be or whether any of us would ever experience life without a chair—we never ever discussed that. We pushed one another and egged each other on, knowing that with hard work and perseverance we each stood a better chance at recovery. We bonded and became friends and cheerleaders for one another.

Once I was more stable, and after reading hundreds of motivating messages from my compatriots back in Massachusetts, the Shepherd Center staff gave my family and me insight into what things were going to be like navigating through life in a chair. Their thorough-but-positive approach allowed me to understand that I may not be in a chair forever. I needed to learn how to maneuver it for now and accept that I will need it for the foreseeable future. They inspired me to work hard and to face this as a challenge. It was truly the first time I understood that with hard work and diligence and future advancements in medical technology that my odds of someday walking again would increase. That's all I really needed to hear to catapult me head first into my next stage of recovery.

One of the first guys I met at the Shepherd Center was a guy named Anton Clifford. Anton became paralyzed at the age of sixteen while a passenger in a car accident. On December 28, 2009, nearly a month before my injury, he was in Jamaica visiting family. Like me, Anton sustained injury to his C4-C5 vertebrae. I'm encouraged by the news that Anton has since regained some movement below his neck and is able to use his arms, but at the time, he was paralyzed from the neck down. Like I do now, Anton used a device called a sip-and-puff to move his wheelchair. Sips and puffs of his breath control his chair. A hard blow makes him go forward, while a hard suck in allows him to go backwards. A soft blow makes him turn right and a soft suck in makes it turn left. We learned that we had a friend in common, so he wheeled down the hall and into my room to introduce himself and offer me his support. Coincidentally, we also learned that we share the same birthday. Two brothers from different backgrounds miraculously joined by a sudden twist of fate. We talked often about how life can change in a minute and how important it is to value every minute with the ones you love. When I met him, I immediately noticed how well dressed he was. He was wearing nice pants, a sharp sweater, and a big old watch on his right wrist. It made me realize that you can still have style even though seated in a wheelchair. This was a big realization for me, as somehow I envisioned myself as an old man, tootling around the streets in my chair. Seeing Anton riding in high style was a really nice feeling for me.

Sadly, Anton learned while in the Shepherd Center that one of his cousins had passed away in the accident. His cousin was sitting right beside him in the backseat. Anton needed someone to lean on, so I tried to step up and offer him support. His positive outlook and huge smile provided me with more support than I was able to offer to him.

I met another guy named Mark Reed a month or so later. Mark, like Anton, had a profound impact on me during my stay at Shepherd. Sometimes people come along in life who teach you valuable lessons or in some way change your life for the better. Anton served as an informal greeter to me, taking me under his wing and helping me feel like I was one of the guys. In turn, I ended up playing a similar role for Mark. Mark entered the hospital looking and feeling a lot like I had done. He was weak looking, forlorn, and appeared to be freezing cold. He was wrapped in towels and blankets and had a look upon his face that showed he was attempting to emotionally process the life changes he was about to experience. I was the first one to welcome him to the floor, just like Anton did for me.

I recalled how scared and alone I felt when I went to the gym for my first time a few weeks earlier. I had wondered if I would be able to break into the clique of guys I saw hanging out and laughing with each other as I wheeled in for the first time. I made friends in no time and quickly became one of the guys. When Mark came into the gym the first time, still wrapped towels and blankets, he looked over at us and appeared to be experiencing some of the same feelings of fear and inadequacy. I called him over and welcomed him to our group of friends. I became his Anton, and in that moment, the torch was passed to the next generation of spinal cord buddies in need.

My early days at the Shepherd Center were extremely challenging physically. My body was just not right, and making the adjustment to life as a paraplegic took its toll. Prior to my injury, I weighed about 155 pounds. After I arrived at the Shepherd Center, I was no longer considered critically sick, but I just could not bring myself to eat. I'm not sure if it was due to some of the medicines I was taking or something physically wrong with my body, but I struggled to get even a granola bar down during the entire day. I fought myself emotionally just to ingest 300 calories a day. It was extremely frustrating for both my parents and me. They encouraged me to eat, but it was as if my desire to take in food was paralyzed too. I later learned that this is a very common event following surgery, but at the time, I was concerned that there was something very wrong with me. It took me fifteen bites to get to the end of a Nutri-Grain bar. I can do that in less than two now. At the end of those fifteen bites, I would beg my mom to throw the rest out and to become my accomplice by telling my father that I ate the entire thing. By the time I was ready to leave the Shepherd Center, I tipped the scales at a dangerously skinny weight of 118 pounds. My body, which was on the skinnier side to begin with, had dropped nearly forty pounds. The aides at Shepherd encouraged me to eat, but had apparently seen enough of this to know that it wasn't as uncommon as I thought and that my appetite would eventually return.

About at the end of March, they tried to wean me off the ventilator. The ventilator controlled my lungs. It breathed for me as it was attached to the trach tube in my neck. I had now been ventilated for nearly two months, and it was important for my recovery to begin breathing on my own. I'm not sure why, but I just couldn't do it. They would take me off the vent for fifteen minutes at a time and allow me to breathe on my own. I seemed to be doing okay but admit to being a bit anxious and apprehensive. I'd start playing games in my mind, and I honestly think that I would cause myself to hyperventilate. So much of recovery is mental. The voice that we all have inside us begins to chatter and we question our ability to perform the things that at one time came so naturally, really simple stuff like breathing and eating for God's sake. These are two pretty essential skills to have in order to maintain life! The staff tried to push me a bit longer with each attempt, but I would be moved to tears. I cried out of frustration at letting down the staff, my family and friends, and most importantly myself.

I failed to wean off the ventilator and was devastated. I was advised that I needed to be back on the ventilator for a few more weeks before trying it again. My mom was bummed, as she really wanted me to not need it anymore. This was a disappointing setback for all of us, but it wasn't the end of the world. I knew at some point, when I was a bit more confident, I would try again and ultimately succeed at learning to breathe without the help of a machine.

CHAPTER 9

I Love that Dirty Water—Boston You're My Home

Day after day passed, and though I was working hard and keeping myself extremely busy, my mind rarely stopped thinking about Meghan. For a mere twenty-four hours before my injury she was officially my girlfriend. We belonged to each other. No one could stake claim to her, and I too was officially off the market. Not that there was a very long line of Norwood high school girls waiting to be my prom date, but it was still a great feeling to know that Meghan could refer to me as her boyfriend.

Because fate would officially pull the rug out from under our maiden scheduled hangout, our first official date took place in my Shepherd Center hospital room. Meghan scheduled a visit down to Atlanta, and I was hyper excited. I wanted everything to be perfect. I laughed at the thought of that. How could I even consider the word "perfect," when I was a thousand miles from home in a hospital bed, with a trach tube protruding from my neck and attached to a ventilator? This was obviously not how either of us had ever envisioned our first date. I suddenly thought back to the phrase "the new definition of normal." This would be how things were going to be moving forward, and the sooner we both accepted it, the quicker it would indeed become "normal."

My dad went out and grabbed us a meal from Wendy's, and it was the first time she fed me. This would give us both a glimpse of what life was going to be like if she made the difficult decision to remain my girlfriend despite the sudden and unexpected change in ground rules. Though I would have expected nothing less from this incredible young woman, Meghan fed me to perfection. She didn't shy away from the uneasy adjustment of having to feed her boyfriend for the very first time. She was comfortable and treated me as if she had been doing this her entire life. I only managed to get down a bite or two of my burger and a few French fries because I was still pretty sick and just not able to muster up much of an appetite. Despite the anticipated awkwardness of our first soiree, things felt very right when she was there. For a second or two, I let my mind wander, and it felt like we were back in Norwood.

Meghan's visit provided a huge boost for my morale and gave me renewed incentive to work hard and recover. She came down with her mother, and it was good to see Mrs. O'Connor, too. It was not that I wasn't giving my rehab 110 percent, but sometimes you need to keep your eyes on the prize and envision what is waiting for you at the end of the long road of recovery. Meghan's visit served as a reminder that a relationship with her was a carrot being held out in front of me to bring me home to the finish line. The visit came at the perfect time. I got to show her around the floor and was able to show her off to everyone. I couldn't help but notice that the guys on the floor shot me a few nods and winks of approval as I brought Meghan into the gym to show her my surroundings.

This was her first time in the Shepherd Center, but Meghan made a valiant attempt to communicate with me every other day prior to her visit. She would send me videos via Facebook Messenger as a way to make us feel like we were together. The videos would last a few minutes as she kept me informed of what was going on at home and how much she was thinking of me. The beauty of her communication was that she would speak to me as if I was answering her back. Unfortunately, I never received them. After being home for about eight months, I finally found them, buried among the thousands of messages of encouragement I had received while I was gone. I discovered the videos and watched them all. Tears streamed down my cheeks and off my chin as I watched one after another for several hours. It was as if I had discovered a treasure chest of love notes. It was a very powerful evening sitting back and watching our love story unfold.

At the beginning of April, a switch flipped and my appetite miraculously returned. Almost overnight, I went from struggling to muscle through a Nutri-Grain bar to wolfing down a foot-long sub with ease. My parents looked at me with a wide-eyed look of absolute excitement as they witnessed me ingesting a full meal for the first time in months. Something just clicked, and I was transformed from a pale and emaciated bag of skin and bone to a perpetual eating machine. I immediately transformed from eating under 300 calories a day to gobbling down over 600 calories a meal. I was somewhat back to normal in this regard. As a kid, my parents joked that everything I ate went straight to the tapeworm and that my epitaph would someday read, "Are you going to finish that?"

I also tried to wean myself off the ventilator again and was able to accomplish this with relative ease. I started by staying off for a half hour, which soon turned into an hour. I was motivated to succeed and pushed myself to stay "vent free" for two hours, then four, and all the way up to sixteen by the fourth or fifth night. My lungs were doing all the work, and I was beyond ecstatic. The sixteen-hour test was supposed to run from 8:00 a.m. to midnight, when the respiratory therapist was scheduled to put me back on the ventilator. Midnight arrived and she never came in. Midnight turned to one o'clock, which turned to two o'clock, and it wasn't until almost three-thirty in the morning that they came in to change it. She felt horrible but explained that there was an emergency on the floor, which caused the delay. Though she was extremely apologetic, my mom and I were ecstatic. I did almost twenty hours of breathing on my own. The next day I pushed it to twenty-four hours and celebrated my accomplishment by symbolically throwing the ventilator away. I was officially ventilator free and fully able to breathe naturally.

This was a huge step for me and for my family. I had been in Atlanta for nearly two months and, day by day, was learning everything about being able to live at home. My parents were learning as well. Very quickly I progressed from struggling to eat and breathe on my own to the point that the conversation began about a return home. After several meetings with hospital staff, it was decided that May 5 would be the day that I would fly home. This decision was obviously met with a sense of nervousness, but overall they were good nerves. There was excitement about being in my house, in my town, with my dogs, my friends, and with Meghan. May 5 would mark 102 days since I had been home. Though it obviously could have been worse, I readily admit that they were the longest 2,448 hours of my life. Not that I was counting. I finally knew that I had achieved a huge milestone in my recovery and was finally able to go home.

Prior to my return, we had to make sure that our home would be transformed into a wheelchair-accessible abode. Like ninety-nine percent of the houses in America, my house was not built for a wheelchair. A lot of work needed to be accomplished in order to transform the Brown Family Home into an accessible facility. Walls needed to be blown out, hallways need to be widened, doorways needed to be expanded, and most of all I needed a way to get into the house. An elevator needed to be constructed to get me from the basement to the first floor. From the very beginning, we knew that major renovations needed to take place if I was ever going to be able to return home. No one ever plans for having to make such accommodations, and the thought of tackling such a full-scale remodel is a pretty daunting task.

As expected, the community came together to ensure that the Brown family was well taken care of; once again showing how great Norwood is. Carpenters and architects volunteered their talents, friends came together to break down walls, pull up rugs, put down hardwood, and generally assist with the remodeling efforts in any

Matt and his aunt, Danni Brown, at the Shepherd Center.

Matt and Meghan before the junior semiformal.

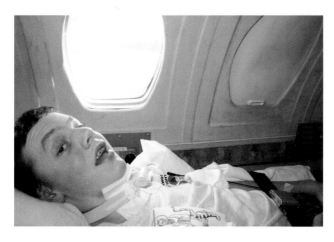

Matt on the flight home from his stay in Atlanta.

Matt and David Ortiz in May 2010.

Andrew Ference giving Matt an up close and personal look at the Stanley Cup.

Boston Bruins defenseman Zdeno Chara and Matt's high school teammates enjoying dinner together.

Local signs showing support for Matt.

Matt and his uncle, Peter Brown, during a learn-to-skate session.

Getting together with friends for the Kentucky Derby.

Matt and Andrew Ference with the player of the game army jacket the Bruins wore.

Matt and his sister Kelley during the holidays.

Matt and Norwood High School principal, George Usevich, after graduation.

The Brown family at Matt's 2016 graduation from Stonehill College.

Matt and his college roommates,
Brian Furey, Zach Wells, Rich Harris, and Nate Soter.

Matt and one of his best friends, Brendan Cathcart,
getting ready for the high school prom.

Skating up the ice during a game sophomore year.

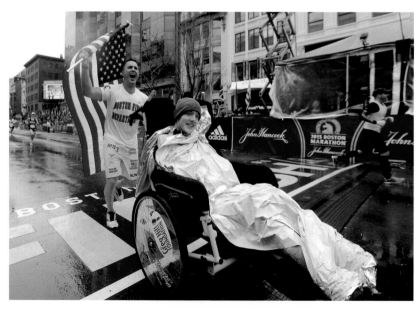

Matt and Lucas crossing the finish line at the Boston Marathon.

*Matt and Lucas Carr nearing the finish line in
the 2015 Boston Marathon.*

*Go Bruins! Matt catching a game with Austin Glaser,
Patrick Lee, and Shannon Brown.*

Matt exits the stage after receiving his college diploma.

Catching up with Patrice Bergeron after a Bruins game.

Matt and Tyler Piacentini pose for a picture at Matt's graduation party.

way they could. The town did an unbelievable job and our home was ninety-five percent complete when I got home. Some of this was funded by my parents, but much of it was via donation of time, talent, and materials. This speaks volumes to the community of Norwood. We rally around each other and support one another when someone is in need.

Along with the big physical changes made to the house, smaller accommodations had to be made in my room, such as getting a bed that was safe for me with bed rails and a mattress that was not too hard. We also had to install an overhead Hoyer lift to get me in and out of bed easily.

I left my home-from-home and said goodbye to the friends and staff who had become my new family. I was transported to the Hartsfield-Jackson International Airport and boarded my own private set of wings back to Boston. Al Bishop and Boston Air Charter One again donated their plane and their services to fly me and my dad back home. One of the coolest things about flying home was that I was able to fly right into Norwood Airport, which is less than a half mile from my house. Norwood Airport is flanked by a large hill, and as we were about to land, we looked out the window and saw that the entire hill was filled with hundreds of people who had come to greet me. Many had signs with my name and "3" on them, and the entire assembly of people were cheering for me as the plane touched down. I looked over to my dad and said to him, "I'm home, Dad."

At the end of the runway, I was greeted by my mom, Kelley, and my dog, Snickers: the most beautiful sight I had ever experienced. Mom and Kelley hugged each other with anticipation as the plane came to a slow, gentle stop. Mom blew kisses to me through the plane window, while Snickers wagged her tail as if she had found a long-lost bone. Mom wore a gray T-shirt with the words "One Goal at a Time" emblazoned on the back. That was the motto we adopted to recognize that we knew improvement would be gradual, but we were committed to setting small but attainable goals.

As I was wheeled off the plane, I was surrounded by microphones and cameras from every local news outlet in Boston and most of the surrounding newspapers. Never one to shy away from the press, I was in my element. The Norwood Fire Department, which had come to bring me home, wheeled me to the fence that stood between the crowd and the runway as the throng of onlookers cheered and screamed my name.

It was important for the townspeople to see me. In many ways, they had suffered through the pain and agony that accompanied my injury, so it was therapeutic to see me come home whole again. I may not be the same physically, but, as I've said many times since then, I'm still Matt. My story was very public. I spent many nights since January 23 in their living room as part of the nightly news, around the dinner table as part of nightly conversation, and even in their bedrooms as part of the prayers they'd recite before calling it a day. They stood with me in spirit during some of the many dark days I encountered, but now they were able to experience a bright day like today as I returned home again.

The Norwood Fire Department loaded me carefully into the back of the rescue vehicle, and together with a second truck (engine number 3, of course), we left the tarmac in convoy. With sirens squealing and horns blasting we made our way through the streets of Norwood before stopping to see my grandmother, who lives just around the corner from us.

My Uncle Paul, a dispatcher for the fire department, was in the back of the truck with me on the way over to see Gram. This was really special to me, as I hadn't seen her since before my injury and she had fallen very sick during my time in Atlanta. My family wanted me to see her before it was too late, so Uncle Paul made the arrangements to stop there before heading home. I asked him on the way over how she was doing, and he just shook his head. The whole visit wasn't long, maybe only a few minutes, but the entire family was there to see it and will remember it forever.

The boys were able to take me out of the ambulance on the stretcher and into Gram's living room. She made her way down the hall from her bedroom, which she had rarely left since she had taken ill. She kissed me on the forehead and said, "I loved the boy who lived down the street. It's so sad what happened to the boy who lived down the street." There was not a dry eye in the room, and that include the firemen who had carried me into Gram's house. She mumbled to me that she loved me and made her way back down the hallway, where she passed away a few days later. I truly believe she held on with all her will just to see me one final time.

After I saw my grandmother, we made our way down to my house, a sight I had longed to see since January 23. So much would have changed since the last time I left my room, a hockey bag thrown over my shoulder, stick in hand, and my future stretching out in front of me. Had it not been for the major renovations that were necessary, I'm sure my room would have looked exactly as I had left it: my bed unmade, dirty sweat socks in the corner, and a half-eaten peanut butter sandwich on my nightstand. It struck me as funny and made me realize how quickly the injury had caused me to grow up. On the morning of January 23, I was an immature underclassman with not a care in the world; 102 days later, I'm faced with grown-up decisions that will have an indelible impact on my future.

Pulling onto our street, we saw cars parked up and down the street, and there were hundreds of people on my front lawn cheering for me as I was moved from the stretcher into the wheelchair that was waiting for me and wheeled into the house. We were able to get settled down long enough to catch my breath and look around the living room before all hell broke loose. Everyone who had gathered outside to greet me, made their way into the house, and we ended up having an impromptu welcome-home party.

All the guests were treated to a tour of our new accommodations. I loved what my room looked like because they knocked down the wall dividing the office and the guest bedroom and made one large room. My palatial room was not only the envy of everyone in my family, but also a man cave for me and all of my friends.

The evening started to wind down as the last guests sensed that I was wiped out after a long flight, a long day, and a very tedious four months. I headed into my room to take it all in. To think. To reflect for a moment. My parents came down after seeing the last guest off, breaking the temporary silence. We looked at each other and said, "Now what?" We collectively shrugged and laughed.

For the next few weeks it was just like that. None of us really knew what we were doing and just learned as we went. We quickly realized there was no nurse to give me meds, to lift me into bed, to clean me up. We were on our own and had no choice but to figure it all out.

The first bed I had looked like it came out of a 1960s mental hospital. It was rock hard with big metal sides. My parents had to flip me over every two hours with pillows to keep me from getting pressure sores. It was an absolute nightmare for the first few weeks. None of us slept through the night, and each of us wondered how we were going to survive. It was like two young parents with a newborn in the house for the first time, trying to figure out shifts and determining who was responsible for what. Soon after, we purchased a nice air mattress bed that circulates me side to side so that I don't need to worry about bedsores. Sleeping on my back was a tough transition, as I had always slept on my stomach or on my side, but, sleeping on my back, like everything else, soon became the norm.

After acclimating to home for a few weeks, I went up to the high school one afternoon to see everyone. I got to see all my teachers and many of the classmates who hadn't seen me since I was wheeled off the ice following the injury. It was great to see their faces, and I'm sure it wasn't half bad for them to see mine either. I was in my wheelchair and was able to demonstrate to the class how to use the sip-and-puff. For the first time since third grade, I was doing show-and-tell, but this time, instead of bringing a frog or a souvenir from a Bruins game, I was showing off my nifty new wheelchair. I demonstrated how the sip-and-puff allows me to maneuver my chair. The kids thought it was pretty cool. I've gotten to the point that I can't envision life without it.

Every night for most of that summer, families from around Norwood would bring over food for us at dinnertime. We didn't need to worry about cooking a meal for about the first four months that I was home. It again speaks to what Norwood is and who these people are. Our downstairs fridge was jammed full of chicken parmesan, spaghetti and meatballs, and lasagna for that entire summer. Trust me, I was not complaining.

On May 23, there was a motorcycle ride that drove through Norwood and ended in Foxboro to raise money for my care. The route took hundreds of bikers right through my neighborhood. I went out to the edge of the driveway and watched motorcycle after motorcycle drive by. They would rev their engines, honk, or give me a wave as they passed me. It was so cool. These were tough yet caring Harley riders who were spending their day raising money for me. Many of them said they had tears in their eyes at the end of the run from seeing me acknowledging them at the end of the driveway.

As awesome as that was, the highlight was that I was finally able to meet Tyler that day. His family came up for a cookout after the motorcycle run. They ended up staying for most of the afternoon. Tyler and I hung out with some of my friends watching the Stanley Cup playoffs on TV. He seemed a bit nervous and very shy, but we got him out of his shell by the end of the day. We talked about hockey but not the injury; I just wanted to make him feel comfortable. I have to give the kid a ton of credit. I'm sure it was unsettling at first to know that his hit, though so innocent, had such an impact on my life. To walk into the lion's den, not knowing how he would be received, took a ton of courage. He likely knew by now that there was no bad blood, but I feel it was still a class act for him to join us. Just as I continued to heal, this was likely a big step in Tyler's healing process as well.

Through the injury, I was obviously thrust unexpectedly into the public limelight. In the weeks and months following the accident, the name Matt Brown was in the news and social media about as often as the BP oil spill and LeBron's *The Decision*. Then, about a week after I got home, the Bruins invited me to one of their playoff games against the Flyers. During the first timeout in the first period, they flashed my story up onto the big screen showing pictures and a voiceover. At the end of the video, they announced, "He is back here today watching the Bruins." They flashed me up on the big screen, and I got a huge roar. That was the first time that I was exposed to the Boston area crowd, and it is a moment I will never forget. I was no longer just Matt from Norwood; now I had become a relatively well-known celebrity in and around New England. It was a position I never dreamed I'd find myself in without being injected with a mysterious dose of hockey talent or good looks, but it was pretty surreal to receive a cheer at The Garden in the same decibel level as Orr, Bourque, and Bergeron.

Even today, when people see me around town, they always give me their best regards. Sometimes it can be in the middle of dinner, when my friends and I or my family are trying to eat. I laugh when people say, "So glad to see you out," as if I was relegated to sitting in my room and hiding away for the rest of my life. I'm still young, and I have a full life to live. That is the positive attitude that I approach each day with.

Many times I am out with either a girlfriend or a friend or two, and we learn that someone has picked up our entire tab or sent a couple drinks our way. On one instance, when my friend Rob and I went out to lunch, someone sent twenty bucks to our table to help pay for our lunch. After a more few minutes passed, we learned that someone picked up our entire tab. We went out to lunch, each had an entire meal, and we ended up making a twenty-dollar profit. It is refreshing to be on the receiving end of such generosity and know there are so many kind people in the world.

CHAPTER 10

A Day Now Symbolized by Hope

By Tyler Piacentini

I started hockey at a very young age and played for many travel teams around the south shore. Every hockey player's dream is to play in the NHL, but that is really hard to do. My dream has always been to simply play at the highest level that I can. I am having fun playing and hope to play professionally for a few years before having to hang up the skates. I would like to get into coaching following my playing career.

Following my graduation from Weymouth High, I played two years of junior hockey for the South Shore Kings in Foxboro, Massachusetts, before being accepted to Norwich University in Northfield, Vermont. I graduated in 2017 while playing hockey and studying communications. During my college career, I was honored to be selected as a captain during my junior and senior year. My brother, Rob, played with me at Weymouth High, and our sister, Melissa, played for Syracuse University. Needless to say we are a real hockey family. While at Norwich, we won a Division 3 National Championship during my senior year, and I was honored to be a finalist for the coveted Hobey Baker Award. I currently play in Huntsville, Alabama, for the Huntsville Havoc of the Southern Professional Hockey League. Despite all of that marginal success on the ice, I'd likely trade it all to reverse that fateful night when I inadvertently assisted in the paralysis of my friend, Matt Brown.

I've relived that play hundreds of times in my mind, and though Matt has likely replayed it even more than that, we both see the play in pretty much the same way. It was a clean play and was unavoidable. One of my best friends, who doubled as my line mate, had the puck coming through the neutral zone with me. It was a two on four coming up the ice. The puck was shot into the corner right next to the net. I was the first one on my team to the puck, and as I got to the goal line I saw a blue jersey. Matt and I collided and bumped shoulders. We both lost our balance, and I saw him career head first into the boards. I immediately knew something was wrong. I got to my feet and Matt didn't. I leaned over and asked him if he was all right. He said nothing, but the look on his face replied a steadfast "no."

I stood on the ice watching with my chin resting on my stick as a Norwood mom and the medical staff tended to him. I knew something was gravely wrong. Many things were going through my mind. What if he's hurt? What if he broke something? The final what-if I feared most—What if he is paralyzed?—was the unfortunate correct question.

It was very tough to finish that game. Both teams were shaken up and contemplated whether or not to complete the contest. We finished and actually won, but the win didn't mean much. Our coach just told us to keep number 3 in our thoughts and prayers.

Following the accident, I had many nights when I had trouble sleeping. Not blaming myself for the hit, but replaying it in my mind with more what-ifs: What if I hadn't bumped him? What if the puck hadn't gone to the end boards? But I soon realized that you can't live like that, and you certainly can't play hockey in that manner. I spent a lot of time thinking about whether he and his family hated me and hoping that they knew it was just an accident. The toughest part was when he was in the hospital, and I had no way of communicating with him. I messaged his sister and his friends on Facebook. I would habitually check to see if they responded. Having patience was tough because I wanted to know how he was doing.

The other Weymouth High captains joined me at a church service that was held for Matt in Norwood. I was nervous, but I knew it was the right thing to do. I met his sister and dad, who gave me a hug and told me that they knew it was an accident. I know it meant a lot to them seeing support from our team there.

I'm not very religious, but I was praying every single day. I understood that the best thing for both of us was to support him in every way possible. I prayed that he would be all right and prayed once he got conscious again that he would respond to my text so that I could apologize and tell him that I prayed for his healing. I also wondered if I was going to get suspended from hockey if it was somehow viewed as a dirty hit. I know what my intent was during the play, but I wasn't entirely sure what it looked like to the outside world. I have never seen a replay of the hit, and I do not ever want to. I heard they showed Norwood the play to make sure people knew it wasn't malicious. Shortly after it happened, I received a few Facebook messages that were not very kind, but my mom had told me to ignore all the negative messages. My parents were very supportive of me and made sure I was all right. They wanted me to be safe.

We ended up playing Norwood again in the playoffs. It was tough for both teams and pretty rough for me. I didn't have the best game. It was a difficult situation playing them because I was really rooting for them. I felt that due to the adversity they had faced it would actually be better if they moved on in the playoffs as opposed to heading home to dwell on Matt.

After Matt returned home that spring, I went to a cookout at the Browns' house with my parents. Although, Matt and I did a lot of chatting through social media and text, I was nervous going. I just wasn't sure how he would react in person, or how I would conduct myself, or how his family would behave upon seeing me at the house. It ended up being a very therapeutic afternoon as I hung with Matt and his friends and they honestly accepted me as one of the guys without any trace of attitude.

In retrospect, the accident has changed me for the better. The way I look at life is completely different. You never know what can happen, and you can't take anything for granted. I have met some incredible people since being an unwitting participant in Matt's life and have made many friends since the accident. Matt and his family are a huge part of that group.

A quote that I have reflected on since the time of the accident is, "The worst thing to happen to you may be the best thing for you if you don't let it get the best of you." Even though that event was one of the worst things to happen to me, I have learned so much from it, and as a result, I have met so many wonderful people. I look up to Matt so much. All of his hard work, perseverance, and positivity is an inspiration to me. Through his sacrifice, I've become a better human being.

When I think back to one of the worst days of my life, I am very fortunate that it is now symbolized by hope. Matt's inspiring personality has taught me the importance of perseverance, community, and forgiveness. I say forgiveness very tenderly because he could have held a grudge against me. Instead, he embraced not only me but also my whole family, and that sums up the type of people Matt and the Brown family are.

CHAPTER 11

Boys Will Be Boys

As the summer wore on, the boys and I began to live life in a way similar to how we always had. Sure, one of us was now in a wheelchair with a trach inserted into his neck, but that wasn't going to stand in between us and the incredible friendship we always shared. As I shared earlier, our friendship group was a lot like the boys in the movie *Stand by Me*, and though we never discovered a dead body by the side of the railroad tracks, we certainly shared some hair-raising adventures together.

In the pre-injury days, we golfed three or four times a week during the summer months. None of us had the responsibility of having a summer job, so we would play nine holes during the morning and mess around the rest of the day. With hardly a care in the world, we would go back to Mark's house to swim, shoot stuff with his BB gun, or blow stuff up with chlorine and rubbing alcohol. We spent weekends with Rob in the town of Dennis, Cape Cod. His family had a compound only a stone's throw from the beach. We were doing what fifteen-year-old boys do; being stupid, but having so much fun.

One of our most unforgettable experiences was the vacation we took the summer prior to my injury. The Dolans had rented a cottage in Falmouth, Cape Cod, where Kyle, Mark, Tyler, and I joined them. We spent hours on the beach, catching rays, scoping girls, throwing a Frisbee, scoping girls, body surfing and, of course, scoping girls.

One time, we decided to partake in the obligatory Cape Cod night, complete with mini golf, go-karts, bumper boats, and batting cages. The grizzled old guy running the go-kart track was being a major jerk, so we put our heads together and came up with a master plan to piss the guy off. We schemed to drive to the farthest place on the track, leave the go-karts running, then to jump over the fence and bolt. We giggled like school girls as we masterminded the great go-kart caper. Mrs. Dolan put the kibosh on our plan when she caught wind of the fact that she was in charge of driving the getaway vehicle after we jumped the fence. Like any well-behaved mother in possession of a strong moral compass, she wouldn't participate in our antics and squashed our master plan. It didn't go down, but it was nearly as much fun planning it out.

The rest of the week, we were in hot pursuit of three cute Jersey girls. We spotted them on the first day and managed to park our towels next to them, valiantly trying to muster the cojones to start a conversation. With our teenage hormones raging, we once again created foolproof plan to get them to notice us. They had perched themselves on the vacant lifeguard stand, so I started screaming and flailing like I needed help. They laughed momentarily but then turned away and continued talking to each other. It wasn't until the last day that we finally got the nerve to talk to them. We hung out the entire day and had a great time. We were pissed that we did not consider just walking up and saying hello the first day. We were just a bunch of socially awkward teenage boys who hadn't yet developed anything resembling maturity or self-confidence around the opposite sex.

The most unforgettable moment of our Cape Cod vacation occurred during a rainy day at the beach. We dug a hole, and I lay in it. The guys then put a blanket over me and sprinkled a bunch of breadcrumbs and chips above me on the blanket. A flock of seagulls landed on the blanket thinking they had struck gastrointestinal gold. I felt them walking across me, and when the boys thought the time was right, they yelled, "Now!" I threw my hands up and grabbed a seagull with the blanket. We did it all afternoon and had the most incredible day being idiots.

Now just a year later, our summertime exploits had become quite a bit different. The guys continued to include me in everything they did, but our choice of activities changed drastically. Forever gone are the days of playing golf, hitting baseballs in the cage, chasing girls on foot, or snatching seagulls. We had to adapt in order to include me as one of the guys. I had literally become the wheel man.

One afternoon, a bunch of us decided we wanted to go see the movie *Inception*, starring Leonardo DiCaprio. At that point in time, I still had the trach in my neck and my parents were very apprehensive about letting me go without them being there too. I had gotten to the point that I needed to be independent, and I really didn't want my parents to be chaperones. No sixteen-year-old wants his parents to accompany him to the movies with the guys, least of all for a film that contains a nude love scene. After a bit of playful arguing and some intense negotiation, my parents came around and agreed to let me fly solo, as long as one of the guys learned to suction out my trach in the event something happened.

When I told the boys, Brendan and Pete stepped forward without hesitation. It's a true friend who agrees to suction mucus out of the hole in your neck just to get you to a movie. Brendan and Pete came over before the movie, and my dad showed them how to do it. They had to take the cover off of the trach, which is called the button. Then they had to turn on the suction and stick a plastic tube inside to suck out the mucus. I could tell that the guys were nervous. My parents were on edge as well, but I was fine. They literally "sucked it up," got comfortable with it, and we were on our way. My mom dropped us off, and as we were making our way from the parking lot into the theater, Pete looked back at my mom and said, "You're not going anywhere, right?" Mom whispered and smiled, "No I will be right here." I'm sure that made both of them feel more comfortable. She suspected that if she was there we wouldn't need her, but if she wasn't around we likely would. That's what is called a mother's instinct.

We sat through the entire movie without incident. It wasn't until we got to the parking lot that I started to get congested. Brendan had a look of slight panic on his face. As promised, Brendan put down the suction machine, took off the valve, cleared whatever was in there, and we were on our way. It showed my mom that I was going to be okay on my own with them, which led me onto the road to more independence. When we go to the movies today, I get to play the role of snack-bar sneak because the guys stick candy, soda, and countless snacks under my chair to avoid the outrageous cost of movie theater treats. There are times that hanging out with your disabled friend can be of advantage.

As the start of the school year approached, I prepared for my return to the classroom. We posted on the website and through social media that I was returning to school. I absolutely refused to bring my parents to class with me, but I needed to find an aide to attend classes, take my notes, feed me lunch and, in general, be my right-hand man. We received a handful of emails from people we knew in Norwood who offered to assist, before receiving one from a guy that we did not know. He sent us a wonderfully heartfelt email that really stood out. We invited him to the house and were awestruck with his immense size when we answered the door; he was so tall and so wide that it was eye-popping. And he had not only the appearance of but also a name that came straight out of English folklore: Wesley Burhoe. Wesley entered our living room and sat down next to me. He placed his gigantic hand on top of mine not even attempting to shake my hand. My mom, Wesley, and I talked about everything we would need, and he made it crystal clear that I would never be in danger. We decided that Wes would be a great fit. I also had a nurse who was at my beck and call during the entire year. Kathleen Clark didn't put up with any of my shit, and we constantly joked with each other.

I still had the trach in my neck, and the school officials were really nervous about it. So in addition to Wesley and Kathleen, my entourage included my mother. Let me make it perfectly clear: I love my mom. I can't imagine life without her. I couldn't ask for a better one. But having your mother accompany you to class every day is no way to go through high school. Mom would sit in the back of the room minding her own business, but people knew she was there, so it was a bit awkward. It was just too much to have my mom hanging out and cramping my style. The trach was due to be removed towards the end of September, so I decided that I would delay my official return to school until the trach was out.

When the trach removal occurred, my world absolutely changed. Whereas nine months earlier, I had so badly wanted a trach to replace being intubated, I was now begging to have it removed. I wouldn't need to worry about it while showering, or it getting hit while getting dressed. My neck would no longer be sore, and the tube wouldn't be getting backed up with mucus. As incredible a feeling as that may have been, the fact that removing meant that my mom didn't have to accompany me to school was the cherry on top. Mom and Dad could just drop me off each morning and go about their own routine. In turn, I had a bit of my independence back.

Though I paid attention in class, I certainly couldn't be accused of spending much of my time at home doing homework. Teachers were very lenient with my grades, and my tests were modified to allow me to ease into the curriculum and learn how to do things in a new way. The administration understood that there was a mental and emotional adjustment to consider as I transitioned from an able-bodied student to one with physical limitations. Though I remained quite popular, there was still a period of coming to the realization that I was no longer a varsity hockey player and would not be able to dance at my junior prom. I was also the only kid in the school who was legally allowed to use the big stall in the men's room. In addition to the emotional adjustment, hockey practice was replaced by daily physical therapy, which was just as strenuous and equally time consuming. When senior year rolled around, the testing modifications disappeared, and

I was required to complete every homework assignment, pass in all papers, and take every test the way it was distributed. It felt good to be a normal student again.

As I began my senior year, the new school opened, and it was absolutely gorgeous. The old high school met the Americans with Disabilities Act definition of accessible, but it was not ideal by any means. In the old school, I could not enter through the front door, the classrooms were tight and the hallways even more so. The elevator was so small that I had to wheel in and sit facing the back wall as we slowly climbed to the second floor. But the new school was state of the art. The hallways were wide, the elevator palatial, and the classrooms large enough for me to do 360 turns, which I did to maneuver but also to entertain my classmates. After a nine-month hiatus, Matt Brown the class clown had returned.

When the hockey season started, I made the decision to return to the rink. Even though I thought it would be therapeutic, the first game was much more difficult than I imagined. I wanted to be out there so badly and really felt an emotional loss while I watched the team from the stands. Before the game began, I went into the locker room to talk to the boys. My heart opened up, and I began to bawl my eyes out. I told them just how badly I wanted to be out there with them, and I encouraged them to play every shift like it was their last. It was pretty apparent that my message was well received as I looked around the room, and there were quite a few tears. As the first period began, we came out flying, and I know that I was the inspiration behind that. Hingham is a powerhouse, though, so we ended up losing, but we played hard.

As I left the locker room, tears were still streaming down my face. I made my way to the corner of the rink, where I would watch every home game for the next two years. My father met me that first game and asked what was wrong. "I just want to be out there with them so bad, Dad," I replied. My dad put his arm around my shoulder and said nothing. I refused to look up at him as I believe that he was crying too.

We both regrouped as warm-ups ended.

In high school hockey, each team's starting lineup is called and, one by one, the players skate to the blue line as they are announced. Forwards first, then defensemen, then goalie. After the goalie is called, the remaining players go out and join the rest of the team for the national anthem. As the team got to the blue line and the anthem started, I ran my eyes down the line. When I got to the end, I saw Austin and Andrew Alty standing next to each other, but there was a gap in between them. That was where I stood. That was how the three of us stood every game. That gap would remain there for the next two years.

Watching got a bit easier, but I know I'll never get to the point that I don't miss playing the game. I will always recognize what I was, even though I don't have any illusion that I was anything special on the ice. I was a third liner on a middle-of-the-pack high school hockey team, unlikely to even play Division 1 hockey. However, like every kid who plays sports, it allows you to dream, to make believe, to fantasize that had you been blessed with a bit more of the talent gene and that, maybe, you could have been the next Bergeron or Ference or Thornton. Losing that dream, no matter how unlikely it may have been, is like having a small piece of me stolen away. Perhaps that is what hurts the most. It's not the physical pain or discomfort that I've had to struggle with the longest, but rather the realization that so many possibilities were stripped away. Though I strongly believe that someday, in the not too distant future, medical science and technology may discover a way for me to regain mobility, there also remains the possibility that I'll never walk down the aisle at my wedding, or dance with my daughter at our first daddy-daughter dance, or beat my son in a foot race. I don't dwell on these things, because it's not who I am, but when the lights go down and I am in bed at night, I'd be lying if I told you that these thoughts don't cross my mind.

CHAPTER 12
My Return to High School
By Wesley Burhoe

My insertion into the life of Matt came quite by accident. My girlfriend's mother was a secretary at the Willett Early Childhood Center and learned that the Norwood school system was looking for aides. It sounded like an interesting opportunity, so I applied. I had no idea that I would be assisting Matt until I was contacted for an interview. I spoke with the people at the school who would be doing the hiring. They informed me that I would need to meet with Matt and his family to make sure I was a fit. I had learned of Matt's accident through the media, but finding myself in his presence felt a bit like I was in the presence of a rock star.

Upon meeting him, I found him to be oddly cool. Oftentimes, when teens are skilled at talking with adults, it's often clouded in a haze of strange. Kids like these are sort of bullshit artists—Eddie Haskell types who don't really understand boundaries. Matt, however, was uniquely different. He was a very confident kid who was clearly raised right. He recognized that he was in a tough position and was going to need help. Matt was trying to find a companion that was laid back and wouldn't be all over him; someone who would try to keep things as normal as possible under his extremely challenging circumstance. I felt as though we clicked in terms of what our goals were. We seemed to have an understanding as to what we expected from each other. I was working for the district but was essentially becoming "Matt's guy." I was paid by the school, but I worked for Matt. I made a personal commitment to be with him until he graduated, as I believed that changing horses in the middle of the race would be considered a setback for Matt. The kid had gone through enough in the past year, and I didn't want to contribute to the upheaval. While the pay was not riches, the experience of being with Matt for six hours a day for nearly two years left an indelible imprint on me as a human being. That is a value that you cannot put a price tag on.

From the beginning, it was clear that the focus was on normalizing Matt's high school experience as much as possible. He had gone through a traumatic event and was trying to get back as much of his life as he could. Matt is super social and has an amazing group of close friends. He was a decent student, so my goals as an aide weren't the same as a traditional aide's. Rather, I was to be the facilitator for Matt to finish his high school career, without his new challenges getting in the way.

Matt's personality is infectious. He is charming and fun and has a way of causing others to forget that he has a disability. Countless times people would reach out to shake his hand without remembering that he no longer has the ability to reach out and reciprocate. Matt plays it off well and everyone laughs, though the moment is accompanied by a slight twinge of embarrassment.

Going back to school was wild for both of us. He was indeed a rock star. Everyone would stop to talk to him, touch him, pat him on the shoulder, and simply want to be around him. The old school had small corridors and only one ADA entrance, so mobility was difficult. It was often stressful because Matt wanted to be as normal as possible, yet would bump into kids in the hall or find himself trapped when a door closed in front of him. The new school, which opened the next year, was a fantastic upgrade. As Matt said, "I can use the front door. I actually feel like I belong here."

Socially, Matt was unaffected. He was himself from the very first moment he returned to school. Physically, he was a shadow of his former self, but emotionally and socially, Matt was still Matt. His ultimate lesson to me and to everyone else who knows him is "always be true." He could have soured or been bitter. It would have been easy for him to recognize the unfortunate hand he was dealt and become a "why me?" pity type. When in public, Matt always succeeded at showing a stiff upper lip; not once did I ever witness him, playing the pity card. Instead, he taught us all lessons in strength, perseverance, and always seeing the glass as half full. I often wondered why bad things happen to good people, and it is evident that it is to allow lesser people to learn valuable lessons through the experience. Matt sacrificed his mobility to teach others to pull the good from life and to refuse to focus on the bad.

Matt was popular enough before he got hurt, but after his injury he was a bona fide super star. Despite his popularity, he stayed grounded and extremely close to his core group of friends. He always had at least one of them in class with him, and while they were focused on academics, they found time to cut up and enjoy each other's company in the classroom. In the minds of his friends or with the school administration, the chair wasn't a problem as much as the medical fears. In case Matt choked while eating lunch, got sick, or passed out from low blood pressure, we had a nurse named Kathleen to accompany us during our first year together. She shadowed us during his junior year. During his senior year, they loosened the reigns, and we simply had to check in with the nurse regularly. I was the only one qualified to feed him his lunch, so we would try to get to lunch early so that he could eat alone without the scrutiny of others. I would then leave him alone while he socialized with his mates. A few times, I broke the rule and would let a friend feed him. It made sense to me since they would do this on the weekends anyhow, and it helped increase their level of comfort if they occasionally fed him at school. His friends made plans to include him in most everything they did. It wouldn't be a shock to see Matt at a girl's hockey game on a Tuesday night with one of his buds feeding him a pizza slice.

Matt did quite well as a student, but all eyes were on him. He was sort of a goofball before the accident, but afterward he was so worried about falling behind that he really worked hard in and out of school. He actually impressed me in with his math acumen, being able to do things in his head that I would have to figure out on the paper. We had some battles when I would say, "That's great you got the answer, but I have to put your work on paper. I can't just write the answer!" Breaking down his thinking and explaining how he got the answer was challenging, but we eventually found a groove. It ultimately helped him become a better writer, as he now writes and speaks incredibly well.

Going back to school was quite a trip for me. It was different than other school aide jobs I've had because I had never supported a student in all subjects. I was Matt's shadow, hanging with him, taking classes right along with him, writing his words and reactions. I tried my best to remain a separate adult, but I was closer to Matt than a teacher or coach would be for two years. I overheard almost every conversation he had, though his friends never made me feel like a weird stalker. I was a necessary part of his high school experience, and his friends did a good job putting up with me. I'd like to think they respected me and the job I had to do.

It was early in my career and, looking back, I wasn't as professional as I wanted to be, but I think it would have been a difficult challenge for anyone. I was one of the guys, but I really wasn't. Matt became like a brother to me, and I believe he thought of me in a similar way. He got what he wanted out of those last two years of high school and captured some of his sense of normality back.

Graduation was a really great experience because I was totally ignored, and that is exactly the way I hoped it would be. I was there to sit next to him, but it was about him. He did it. "We" didn't accomplish anything. I'll acknowledge that I helped in some areas and we were a team, but it was his team.

After graduation, it was a real transition for me; like closure in many ways. Matt's father referred to me as one of the family, and that makes me extremely proud. It was a very gratifying moment for me to see Matt accomplish what he had set out to achieve. The Browns are a big group of caring and funny people, and to be accepted by them is a high honor. I was happy to slowly fade into the background as Matt got the recognition and praise he deserved.

I've not really stayed in touch with them aside from an occasional Facebook post, but they are still a huge part of me. They helped me learn what real adversity is. I now know what real courage is. I know what persistence is. Most importantly, I know what friendship is. I know what unconditional love looks like. I saw it all up close. When you see something real, it stays with you.

I miss hanging with Matt. He's getting older, so maybe our paths will cross again someday. Regardless, I love him and don't know if I can truly articulate how much my time with him changed me for the better. I'm honestly a better person for having spent two years of my life in his presence.

CHAPTER 13

Is There Life After High School?

"Great moments are born from great opportunities."

— Herb Brooks

The school year came to a close, and I realized that summer was going to be kind of tough. During the first summer following my accident, everything was fresh because I was spending most of my time getting used to new routines. My friends and their families and even soon-to-be friends were at the house constantly, showing that they cared and checking in around the clock to see how I was doing. I was busy all the time and was even a bit overwhelmed at times because my calendar was full to boiling over.

The summer following my junior year was the opposite and served as a bit of an eye-opener. There is no doubt in my mind that people still cared, but visits became less frequent, and my injury was no longer considered a hot topic around Norwood. I had to work to find things to keep me busy, and I spent many days in my room bored out of my mind. There were times when the boys or Meghan and her friends would spend the day at the beach, and I was stuck at home. Pushing a wheelchair through the hot, thick sand at Rexhame Beach is not very high on anyone's to-do list. I'd often meet up with crew after they got back, but it was tough listening to the stories of their day at the ocean, while I was forced to live vicariously through their experiences.

I speak with my family and my friends frequently. Without such a close-knit and generous group that surrounds me, I honestly don't know where I would be. I never expect them to feel sorry for me, but I do lean on them for emotional support, and they have helped me to understand that it is very normal to see the glass as half empty now and then. I try valiantly to focus on the positive every day, and the good days undoubtedly outnumber the bad, but there are many times when I struggle. I often sit and ponder how the best years of my life were sacrificed by an unfortunate twist of fate. There are some days when I sit in my room and wish I wasn't here. That sounds like a pity party, and it pains me to print it for the world to witness, but it's the truth. Not being able to play hockey, not being able to treat Meghan the way she should have been treated, or not being able to be that obnoxious teenager I was destined to be takes a mental toll on me. I always considered myself to be extremely independent growing up. My parents encouraged Kelley and me to do things on our own, to make decisions like adults, and to learn and grow from those decisions. Having that sense of independence ripped from you is a tough pill to swallow, and though I've managed to find the best in most situations, there are many days where reality gets the better of me.

There are plenty of times I haven't gone out with my friends because I feel like it's a hassle to make the necessary accommodations to include me. Loading me into an accessible vehicle, feeding me a meal, having to sit in the handicapped section of a movie theater or sporting event is not how most people want to spend a night out. It's not fair for my parents to get woken up in the middle of the night or sacrifice their golden years to take care of their son. All in all, I know that I'm luckier than many and have been afforded many opportunities as a result of my injury, opportunities that both able bodied or disabled people would give anything to experience. It's not lost on me that being a recognizable figure in and around Massachusetts, becoming the adopted son of the Boston Bruins, spending the day with the Stanley Cup, being able to complete the Boston Marathon on several occasions, and so many more incredible opportunities, are gifts that I have experienced. Having the ability to inspire and lift up others and affect their lives in a positive manner far outweighs these negative days that creep up on me now and then. That doesn't mean that every day is full of bright sunshine, though.

Meghan and I spent a lot of "us" time together and become more comfortable with every moment we shared. She now had her driver's license, so we would often go do our own thing without friends or parents in tow. We never suffered from boredom when we were together. Whether enjoying dinner out, a movie, or just a drive, we were your typical high school couple. The summer following graduation, my family went on a cruise with a couple of other families, and Meghan joined us. I was still absolutely head over heels in love, and I know that Meghan felt the same. Though our relationship was physically challenged, we would lie in bed and cuddle together while watching a movie. We both dealt with the limitations as well as could be expected, and this became another example of the new normal.

I often wondered if Meghan was happy with the way her life had changed nearly as much as mine had. Did she really care for me at the level that I cared for her? Or was she caught in sort of an uncomfortable predicament? I feared that she was concerned about how it would look to others if she broke up with me. I feared that she had decided to simply tolerate the baggage I came with. I had a long, deep conversation with my mom one night and told her that I was thinking of breaking up with Meghan. I thought that it may be best for me to pull the trigger before she did. I told Mom that all of this was too hard on Meghan and that I should do her a favor by breaking things off. "Are you sure you want to do that?" she asked me. "This might be hard on her, but she's a strong girl. I think she's doing okay with it, and I think she is very important to you." Once again my mother knew best. I actually told Meghan about the conversation about a year later, and she got extremely choked up. She said to me, "Matt, I have no intention of leaving you. I care about you and love you for you." That was really important to hear and extremely reassuring to me. It also reminded me what a wonderful person she is.

As senior year began, I realized that my teen years as I knew them were coming to an end. It's difficult to explain, but from January 23, 2010, to the very moment I had this epiphany, my entire focus was on the injury, the recovery, how to fit in with those around me, and how to cope with the here and now. Life had flown at me so rapidly, and I had been so consumed with the recovery, that I had honestly not thought one single minute about what I was going to do after high school. It had totally escaped me that once senior ended and the doors of Norwood High closed behind me for the last time, that I was faced with the reality of adult life. What the hell was I going to do? Had my long-term goal of going to college after high school been aborted? All my friends were talking about going on to college and were even beginning to apply, but I had not once even considered the logistics of making the jump from living in my parent's basement and being accompanied to class by Wesley to life as a college student.

I burst through the door one day after coming home from school and announced to my mom and dad that I had decided to go to college. They looked at each other with a puzzled expression. They then simultaneously looked at me like I had three heads, but not because they were surprised that I had decided to go, but rather that I was even considering not attending. Though the road may have had a temporary detour, it had not hit a dead end. Their reaction was comforting and actually catapulted me into full-fledged college admissions mode.

My aunt Trish began coaching women's basketball at Stonehill College in Easton, Massachusetts in 2001. She has held the position for the past seventeen seasons, and is a four-time Northeast-10 Conference Coach of the Year. Aunt Trish is a legend not only at Stonehill but also in the lore of women's college basketball. Entering the 2018 season, her career winning percentage placed her fifteenth among active coaches in Division 2 and thirty-first all-time in Division 2. I had been going to see her games since I was in first grade, and from that very young age I loved Stonehill College. At the time, they were the Chieftains and not the Skyhawks, and the campus looked much different back then. A road cut straight through the middle of campus and past the gymnasium as the Shield Science Center was still many years away. The campus was vibrant and beautiful. In the years that followed, our family would take many trips to watch Aunt Trish and the women's team play. She's one of eight children, so our section was always lively. During these trips, I began to explore the campus and started to think about what it would be like as a student at Stonehill College. As I got older, my personal commitments prevented me from being able to attend as many games as I would've liked, but Stonehill's appeal was still present. When Aunt Trish heard I was going to apply to the very school where she has amassed over 300 victories, she reached out to the dean, the president, and the department of academic services to see if she could grease the skids for her nephew. Without the need for even a speck of favoritism, we were invited to the school for a meeting, and I was welcomed with open arms. They greeted me as if I was either the Norwood High valedictorian or a prized athletic recruit, not a B-student class clown or a third-line hockey player in a wheelchair. Not that it would take much persuasion, but they sold Stonehill to my parents and to me and asked what accommodations I would need in order to attend. It stood out to my parents and made them comfortable that I was going to be okay. It made me feel like the school really wanted me.

One of the most important issues they conveyed to me was that I did not need to complete my degree in four years. This allowed me the peace of mind to ease into freshman year with a lighter workload. I assume that every incoming freshman, regardless of their situation, is a bit insecure as to what lies ahead. Due to my unique situation, this was especially comforting, and it reassured me I had not chomped off more than I could chew. At Stonehill, I sensed that I would be treated like a living, breathing student with a name and not just a number. The community seemed to be incredibly close knit.

I applied to other schools just to say that I had, but Stonehill was the only place I really wanted to attend. It was my first choice, my stretch school and my safety school, all wrapped into one. Not that my grades were anywhere near good enough, but I actually applied to Harvard as a joke. About two or three weeks after I applied, they called me for an in-person interview. I thought, *Oh shit, what did I do?* Someone came to our house. We talked about the classes I had taken in the past and my goals for the future. The interviewer was extremely intelligent if not a bit short on personality, and I was honored just to have them there. You can bet your ass that I framed that rejection letter.

When the acceptance letter came from Stonehill, I was ecstatic. I kept saying, "Wow! I'm really going to college." This was just as quickly followed up by the reality that, once again, we had to figure out the logistics of how to make it work. Though Easton is only a half-hour drive to Norwood, I decided even before I received the acceptance letter that I really wanted to live on campus. It was going to take quite a sell job, as I assumed my parents would have trouble seeing their little boy leave the nest. They were just the opposite and encouraged the idea. I joke with them that they started packing up my room months before school was ready to start. In a way, it's understandable. Parenting me 24/7/365 hasn't been a walk in the park for them, and shipping me off to college would likely give them much-needed recuperation time.

In the spring leading up to graduation, Coach Igoe asked if I wanted to help out with the baseball team. I was all in. I attended nearly every game and served as a combination bench coach, cheerleader, and good-luck charm. Being on the bench with the guys and participating as a member of the team was a gratifying experience, and though it will never replace my love for hockey, it was a great opportunity.

On the same day Norwood lost in the South sectional semi-finals in hockey, I was honored at a Bruins game by dropping the ceremonial puck at center ice. The Boston Bruins Foundation actually bought my wheelchair for me, so it was an opportunity for them to honor me while also showing off the chair. My dad and I took to the ice via the "black carpet" with former Bruin and current director of the Bruins Foundation Bob Sweeney. We met with Zdeno Chara and the captain of the Islanders at center ice. As I rolled to center ice and my name was announced, I looked up in the stands. The crowd rose to their feet and roared at a level that I had never before experienced. It made me once again realize how lucky I was to have been loved and admired by so many whom I had never even had the pleasure of meeting. They cared about me and wanted nothing more than to witness my continued recovery. It was therapeutic for the fans who had prayed for me to see me at the greatest place in the world: center ice at The Garden. As we were coming off the ice and about to cross the blue line, I looked at my dad and said, "You know what just happened? I think I blacked out." It was definitely one of the highlights of my life.

When senior prom came around, Meghan wore a long gray and pink prom dress that left not only me but also most of the guys at the prom absolutely drooling. She looked stunning. She wanted me to wear a gray suit with a pink tie to match her dress. However, the rather flamboyant salesman at the tuxedo store wouldn't hear of it. He set me up with a black tux and assured me that I was going to look just as stunning. It was the first time I had ever been fitted for any suit, and being in a chair made it a bit challenging for both of us. Mom made sure we did all the measurements while I was lying down in bed. We had the tailor put an extra inch or two on the pants so that when I sat down it didn't look like I was waiting for a flood.

Everyone met at the gazebo in the center of Norwood and took pictures. This is a Norwood High tradition. All the couples boarded trolleys that took them into Boston for a dinner and party. We found a wheelchair-accessible trolley so that I could participate, which was absolutely awesome. Unlike any of the others, our car had strobe lights and music, making us the envy of all the others. We took pictures with my jacket on, and then before boarding the trolley, I had my dad take the jacket off, and I just went in my tie and vest. The day after prom, we all went down to Rob's family's compound in Dennis, the ideal place for about twenty-five of us to spend the weekend.

I can't really say what I view as my greatest life accomplishment to date. Making it back to school at all was huge for me, especially because that possibility hung in perilous balance just a few months earlier. Getting accepted to Stonehill and finishing my first Boston Marathon are events that I am extremely proud of. Graduating from Norwood High, however, fills my chest with the most pride and feels like the very greatest of all my achievements. I had hung with most of my class since the age of five or six, and the thought of not accepting my diploma with them had really haunted me. In the end, graduation was to be an event we all experienced together and thinking of having Mark, Pete, Kyle, Rob, and Austin walk across the stage while I was left behind would have been an excruciatingly difficult. It would have been like seeing all your friends board the bus for a field trip, leaving you at home nursing a cold.

I was very happy and very proud of myself that I got there. I know it wouldn't have been possible without the help I received from my family, my teachers, the administration at Norwood High, my friends and, of course, Wesley and Meghan. But this accomplishment was about me and my effort to make it happen. It was an accomplishment that wouldn't have taken place without diligence, perseverance, commitment, and my refuse-to-quit mentality. Despite my relatively mediocre grades, I'm not stupid enough to forget that I made this happen. I could have easily rolled over and ended my schooling on January 23, 2010, with the assumption that would be my "get out of jail free pass." What teenager wouldn't love to receive a note from his mom that said, "My son will not be in school today"? I wouldn't hear of that though. My education did not end when my body broke, and it was more important than ever to value the opportunity of education that we are all afforded. Completing high school, and ultimately college, was not optional in my mind.

Graduation day was unbelievable. It was an afternoon I will cherish forever, and I am overjoyed I was able to attend. But in addition to graduation, I also received a "golden diploma." The golden diploma is given to students who overcame serious obstacles in completing their high school careers. Previously, the award was given to a young woman named Michelle Kennedy, who had battled leukemia before succumbing to the illness. I guess it can't be argued that the obstacles I overcame would fall into the category of serious!

Receiving my regular diploma was incredible as well. Graduation was held on the football field, and rolling across the track to receive my diploma from Mr. Usevich was a moment to behold. Mr. Usevich was one of my biggest cheerleaders and the principal of the high school. He is a man that absolutely loves the town of Norwood and adores each and every young adult who attends the high school. To receive my diploma from a legend like George Usevich was extremely emotional for me. I looked into his eyes as he placed the diploma in my lap, and his eyes were filled with tears. I could tell that he was proud of my accomplishment and knows that he had a major role in helping me achieve it. Nothing about that day could've been better. It was the first big milestone I was able to cross off of my list.

The Friday before graduation, the school had Class Day. This is the day when seniors go into the auditorium, with parents in attendance, and many of the school awards and scholarships are handed out. This was the first year of the Matt Brown Annual Scholarship, an award presented to a male or female senior hockey player based on a written essay they must submit. The topic of the essay is motivation, determination, and perseverance. I was able to read all of the essays, and they were each incredible in their own way. The essays had the names blacked out to make it both fair and easier on me. I couldn't be biased based on any known connection to the author. Nevertheless, I ended up picking Brendan's essay. It was a really special piece of writing and doubly special that he turned out to be the author. He was the friend that I had called onto the ice to tend to me when I was hurt. Now, in a way, I was able to take care of him.

As for me, I won an award named after my mom's Uncle Tom and her cousin Jeff Brown. Jeff died at a young age and the Jeffrey Brown Scholarship was created in his honor. Being named the winner made it incredibly special, and Mom was equally thrilled.

Meghan would be off to Springfield in the fall, while I was off to Stonehill. She graduated with a basketful of honors in high school and had decided to major in occupational therapy. When I see her father, he says, "You know, Matt. You might've just had something to do with that." My relationship with Mr. O'Connor had come a long way since the days of busting balls at the Little League field.

One thing that really fills me with a sense of pride is learning how many people wrote their college entrance essays about me. There was a time in my life that they could only write about a third-line center and class clown who was relatively ordinary. Instead, they had chosen to write about the kid, who despite some challenges, had found a way to become quite a bit more than ordinary. It was really special to look in the mirror and realize that through my adversity, I was having an impact on the lives of others. I know that I'm still just Matt, but maybe "just Matt" has found a way to enhance the lives of others in ways other than simply spouting out a well-timed joke.

CHAPTER 14

Bittersweet Milestone for Matt Brown

A few days after my graduation, writer Scott Barbosa of ESPN.com penned a story titled "Bittersweet Milestone for Matt Brown," which shares the story of that special day. It is extremely well-written and remains the fondest recap of such a momentous occasion. He has graciously allowed me to share his story here.

> NORWOOD, Mass. — By the time Matt Brown left the football field behind Norwood High School on Sunday there wasn't a soul left to ask him for a picture. The chorus line of well-wishers with their refrains of "Congratulations!" fell silent. The few who remained were workers clearing the foldable chairs and staging from the track area.
>
> In one end zone, Matt's parents, Mike and Sue, and an aunt waited for him underneath the goalpost.
>
> Matt says that graduation day is more about them—his family—than anything else, though you get the sense that "family" applies to more than flesh and blood. From the time the Class of 2012 lofted caps into the air until he met his family underneath the goalpost, a cavalcade of people who've lifted Matt during the past two-and-a-half years heaped praise on him.
>
> The first to visit Matt was his girlfriend, Meghan O'Connor.
>
> On Jan. 23, 2010, Matt, then a sophomore, broke his fourth and fifth cervical vertebrae during a varsity hockey

game against Bay State Conference rival Weymouth, leaving him paralyzed. That day has forever altered Matt's life. But the previous day, Jan. 22, his life changed as well. It was the day he asked Meghan out on their first date.

She was present among the welcome crew in May 2010 when Matt arrived at the airport after spending 102 days at an Atlanta rehabilitation center. She has been by his side throughout, although they will be separated by distance next year. Meghan will study occupational therapy at Springfield College, while Matt will attend nearby Stonehill College.

"I'd like to think I've had an impact on her wanting to study that," Matt said.

Throngs of people moved in on Matt, whose persona in Mustang-land is one part rock star, one part politician. A host of his hockey teammates weaved in and out before the group banded together for one last team picture.

Mustangs hockey fell in the Division 1 South semifinals, pinched out in a 1–0 loss to Natick. Matt noted their tournament run as a highlight of his senior year. He was in attendance for all of the Mustangs' playoff games and a fixture at the rink throughout the season. Norwood head coach Bill Clifford gave Matt a de facto assistant coach's role with the team, noting that he took Matt's observations to heart as his "second pair of eyes."

"He sees things that I miss down on the ice," Clifford said during the hockey season. "He knows the game well."

As the group gathered around Matt for a photo-op, Norwood teacher and assistant football coach Wesley Burhoe spoke of Matt's sense of humor. It's a large part of what makes him so endearing to so many. Burhoe became particularly close with Matt since his return to high school. Serving as a "set of hands" for Matt in his time at the school, Burhoe estimated they've spent about 2,000 hours together.

"The best part about him is, today, he comes up to me and tells me that he loves me," Burhoe shared with head football coach John Sarianides while looking back at Matt. "That just got me."

Burhoe was part of an extensive support team that made Matt's transition back to the high school possible. When Matt returned to school in May of his sophomore year, the old building wasn't properly equipped for his wheelchair. Matt came in through a back entrance to the school, and each day he was greeted by Principal George Usevich.

Norwood's new high school building is accessible by wheelchair from the front entrance. Usevich remained the first person Matt saw in school each day.

Matt received one of three Golden Diplomas handed out by Usevich on Sunday, recognizing students who overcame serious obstacles in completing their studies.

"You're not going to find a more special kid than Matt," Usevich beamed.

Matt continued through the seemingly endless receiving line, with kisses on the forehead from guidance counselors and hellos from parents of fellow students.

"I don't know if you remember me," one hesitant mother approached Matt.

"Of course, Mrs. Wong!" Matt shot back. "So nice to see you."

While Matt is enrolling at Stonehill undeclared, he's leaning toward business. He has hinted to his mother that he would like to try his hand at sports broadcasting, too. No matter the application, his natural warmth with people is something that will translate to whatever he endeavors.

"[My mom] tells me all the time that I can't be all over the place all the time," Matt said. "I have to focus on one thing at a time."

It's that attitude, coupled with his competitive streak that has pushed Matt in his recovery.

The fall will bring change for Matt and his family. He plans to stay on-campus at Stonehill. The Browns' morning routine will no longer involve getting Matt ready for school, starting at 6:20 each morning. With change comes independence, and his dream is that one day he will find ultimate independence in regaining the ability to walk.

Until then, Matt has found success in the small victories: finding movement in his left arm, wrist and his fingers; the wiggle of his toes; the lifting of a thigh. He got himself back in the classroom, when others might have faltered. He graduated on time. He's going to college.

It's everything others might take for granted. It's everything that makes Matt an inspiration to everyone he touches.

He talked about his two-hour physical therapy sessions three days a week at Journey Forward, a nonprofit organization in Canton.

"They're going to be the people that get me out of this chair," Brown says defiantly, his eyes locked in conviction.

He described his graduation day as bittersweet; proud of his accomplishment, he was going to miss seeing his teammates every day in the hallways.

"Things change and you all move on, but what I've developed with my teammates in the last couple of years, that's never going to change," Matt said.

He wheeled over to his family and they started toward the exit, nearly an hour past the end of the ceremony. The party would continue at home.

Thing is, Matt Brown will never leave Norwood High School.

CHAPTER 15

My Life as a Stonehill Skyhawk

Aside from academics, my time at Stonehill provided me with the perfect medicine I needed—a sense of independence. Mom and Dad certainly granted me the space I needed, but they were also at ease knowing I was just a long stone's throw away. Villa Theresa was my dorm freshman and sophomore year. I lived on the first floor with Austin in a room that was actually intended for three. It was spacious and roomy enough for my chair, so it was the perfect living arrangement.

Sharing my college experience with Austin was incredible, and I couldn't have asked for a more supportive and understanding roommate. Austin had gone back and forth on whether to attend Merrimack or Stonehill. I was thrilled when he decided upon Stonehill, and more excited when it became apparent that he and I would be roomies. We roomed together all four years, which I have to give Austin credit for. Though we were and remain best friends, rooming with me comes with additional duties above and beyond the job description of typical college roommate. Austin didn't seem to mind that he had to play the role of nursemaid at times. He often joked that he would have rather had a roomie he could play video games with, but aside from that we did just fine. Friends would often ask Austin what it was like taking care of me, when in truth I was usually the one taking care of his sorry ass.

I had a going-away party circled on the calendar for Friday night, as classes were to begin on the following Tuesday. Several of my buddies who were still local, came over to hang along with Meghan, Mom, Dad, Kelley, and numerous members of my extended family. Though the night was awesome, I could feel the nerves in my stomach throughout most of the night. Leaving home and living at school is a big change for any college-bound teen, but for me it added more stress. As the night ended, Meghan and I went upstairs to say goodbye to one another, and we both got pretty emotional. We had been going steady for so long and had been through so much that it really made us grow up. She was my best friend and the first girl I fell in love with. Though we were not moving to other side of the world from each other, I knew that the transition to life as a disabled college freshman was going to be made more difficult without having her by my side.

Saturday morning, I woke up and my stomach was in knots. My parents brought me to Stonehill, helped set up my room, said goodbye, and my college career was officially underway. A few days went by, and I was really struggling. Only forty-eight hours into my college career, and I was absolutely sure that I had made the wrong decision. I was homesick and sensed that I was going to have the word "dropout" next to my name before long.

A "Welcome Cookout" was arranged as a way for new students to get to know each other more. Austin and I wolfed down some burgers and dogs and introduced ourselves to a few people before deciding to head back to the dorm. The cookout was at the top of a hill, so we proceeded down the driveway. As we got to the sidewalk, I struggled to hit my emergency brake button with the side of my head. I finally coordinated my efforts and stopped my chair just as I reached the road. A car buzzed by, the driver not even tapping his brakes, and nearly sideswiped my legs. Austin and I looked at each other wide-eyed, realizing how close that car came to taking out my legs. I'm not 100 percent certain, but I think we both may have peed our pants a bit. It was a really close call. That is no way to begin your college career.

As we went through the back door of the dorm, the side of my chair nicked the wall. I must have caught it just right because the tube that carries the air from my mouth to the control panel, which is how I control the chair, broke in half. I could not do anything to move my chair, which weighs about 375 pounds. I was stranded. I asked Austin to switch the settings so that he could control the chair from the manual joystick that sits behind me. Now, this is no video game. The joystick is very tricky. Pushing it up makes the chair go up while pushing it down makes the chair go down. When you push the joystick left, the back of the chair spins right and vice versa. It must have taken us about twenty-five minutes to get me down the hallway to our room, which is about thirty feet away.

We got to our room and reassessed the situation trying to regain our emotional footing before attempting to MacGyver a solution. Austin found where the break had occurred and got to work. We found a roll of duct tape, and with the help of another guy who stepped in to help, we began to layer the tape. I would occasionally test it to see if it resolved the issue before they would layer on more where it needed to go. After about ten minutes, we were up and running.

I look back at this as a monumental event. I had been at school for only about four hours. I had just said goodbye to my parents in a show of independence before nearly being sideswiped by oncoming traffic and almost decapitated by wheelchair. I thought about calling my parents to come back down to fix the chair, but instead we took it into our own hands. We assessed the situation we found ourselves in and figured out a big-boy, grown-up solution instead of relying on Mommy and Daddy to wipe our eighteen-year-old asses. We found ourselves in similar situations during the next four years, and a large majority of the time we figured it out. We were growing up before our very own eyes.

Riding around campus in my chair, many students would look at me with curiosity. The first thing people try to assess is whether I can speak clearly. I don't see this as being judgmental because it is often challenging to begin a conversation with someone who is speech impaired. Many people may shy away from an initial encounter for that reason. I try to show people that there's nothing to be nervous about. All it usually takes is starting a conversation with them and they realize that I am no different at all. I let them know that I just walk on four wheels.

The tentative reaction of students soon dissipated, and I realized that Stonehill was a great spot for me after all. As the nephew of the women's basketball coach, it seemed that the entire girls' team was looking out for Austin and me. We were frequently invited to hang out with them, and they got us into all the parties. Through their introductions, we met many people and eventually got close with the hockey team, becoming friendly with Brendan, Kevin, Chris, Fabio, Ollie, and a kid we only knew by the name of Cheese.

The first month or two of school wasn't without its challenges. My parents had to travel down every morning and night to get me in and out of bed. This was really tough on them, but a chore that comes along with having a disabled son. They'd wake up early and get home late at night like they were the parents of a newborn. It really hurt me knowing that their life had been turned upside down as a result of my misfortune. It's a reality that they were forced into but committed to graciously. They continued this daily practice until we had nurses or aides set up who could help me get my day going and allow them to sleep in. I'd much rather have my parents get a good night's sleep and an easy morning then to play the role of personal care attendant, but for the first few months they rolled with the punches and did what they had to do to get me ready for school.

As women's basketball coach, Aunt Trisha was friendly with the men's hoop team as well. Patrick Lee was a graduating senior and was soon to become an assistant volunteer coach for the men's team. He needed to find a side job that would pay him in addition to his volunteer role. Trisha knew Patrick and believed he would be a perfect fit to assist me in my daily routine. Dad and I met him and agreed that Patrick was exactly who I needed. We let Pat know that we were going to need someone to take me to physical therapy, walk me to and from class, and head over to the cafeteria to feed me. During my junior year, he decided that coaching wasn't for him so he hung out with me all day. He would drop me off and come back to hang out in the suite with the rest of the guys.

Austin and I made a ton of friends once we got comfortable with our new college surroundings. Jess, Pat's girlfriend at the time, played for the women's lacrosse team, and she introduced us to rest of the team and all the women that they lived with. All in all, Austin and I became pretty popular, and we didn't have much to worry about on campus.

Meghan and I entered our respective freshman years as a long-distance couple. We knew this would be difficult for any couple to sustain but made the mutual decision of trying to stay together. We talked nearly every day about classes, acclimating, and the new friendships we had both made. During Columbus Day weekend, all the college locals go home to take a breather from school and to get reacquainted with our high school friends. I was at my buddy Mark's house on Friday night hanging with all the boys. Meghan stopped over with some of her friends. I could tell something was wrong and mentioned it to the boys after all the girls left. I saw the writing on the wall.

We went out to dinner in Boston the following Saturday night, and everything seemed to be okay. On the ride home, however, she was especially quiet. We got to my house and lay down together. I asked her what was wrong and she didn't say a word. She started to fidget. I said, "You don't love me anymore, do you?" She didn't say a word and just looked at me. I could see it in her face as she struggled to find something to say. For that very moment, I felt as though this was worse than losing my ability to walk, play hockey, or feed myself. Losing those very important abilities was an accident. Losing Meghan was a choice. We exchanged a few uncomfortable words back and forth before I told her, "I have nothing to fight for anymore. I have nothing to work towards anymore." The words were harsh and perhaps a bit selfish, but that was how I felt at the time. She got up and left.

I just lay there and stared at the ceiling for hours. I didn't know what to do, so I finally called for my mom. I was a mess. I told her that Meghan broke up with me. I was really hurt and felt really alone. Though it was apparent that it was what we needed to do, it knocked me on my ass. However, like my injury, I eventually picked myself off the ice, without assistance this time, and learned another new definition of normal. Meghan still remains one of my friends, and we care about each other very much. I'm still working towards my goal of walking again and think of her as a positive affirmation when I work in the gym and the rehab facility. I want her to do well in her future vocation as an occupational therapist, and I know my injury helped nudge her career in that direction.

We grew up together and were forced to mature very quickly. This wasn't just your typical high school crush coming to a typical close. It was more than that. Meghan got me through some of the darkest moments in my life. She was there to pull me out when I was at my lowest. For that I'll be forever grateful.

After freshman year, I visited my buddy Sam Anderson at his home. A bunch of the guys were there watching a Bruins game in his basement. The house wasn't wheelchair accessible, so there was no way I could get the chair downstairs. They brought me into the garage and devised a plan. One guy wrapped his arms around my chest and lower abdomen, while the other grabbed me under my legs. They carried me into the basement like a potato sack and tossed me onto the couch. We watched the entire game, enjoying a few beers and watched the B's win. I couldn't have felt more like one of the guys.

During our first two years at Stonehill, I lived in Villa Theresa, which was strictly a freshman and sophomore dorm. When it came time for junior and senior years, Austin and I wanted to stay with kids our age. There were some hockey kids who were looking to get a suite. We had become close with them and discussed becoming part of their herd. There were seven rooms in each suite to house fourteen guys. Need I say more? These were the two best years of my life at Stonehill. We had so much fun, featuring more belching, farting, guzzling, and guy-talk then you could ever imagine. I admire each of them for accepting me as they did and for never thinking twice about choosing to live with a guy in my situation.

One Saturday night during our senior year, everyone started to make their way home to the suite after a night out on campus. We started off playing drinking games and cards in the common room and eventually found ourselves surrounded by empties. One of the guys started to stack them on the table into a Jenga-like tower of beer cans. My buddy Evan spied the "Heaping Tower of Hops" and you could see his wheels start to turn as he conjured up the world's most incredible grand finale. When I was in high school, I had received a football helmet signed by Dwayne "The Rock" Johnson after his role in the movie, *The Game Plan*. Evan went into my room and came out wide-eyed, wearing the helmet. The entire room of half sauced hockey players went nuts. Everyone took the pillows off of the couches in the common room and put them up against the wall at the end of the hallway. We moved the can tower in front of the pillow wall and Evan ran to the opposite end of the hallway and then stood like a mad bull ready to charge. We all gathered around and counted down like we were in an abbreviated scene from Times Square on New Year's Eve. Evan took off and raced down the hallway sporting a devious grin visible through the bars of The Rock's helmet. He leaped about a foot away from the table into mid-air and crashed into the beer can tower, helmet first. He took out every can in his path before landing safely in the pile of pillows. As you can expect, the room erupted in a loud and raucous cheer. Mic drop!

When the boys, wanted to go out on the town they would usually check in advance to determine whether or not I could get into whatever location they'd chosen. This eventually evolved into "Let's not ask. Let's just do whatever we have to do to get him in." Of course, hanging out with me comes with its own set of "elimination responsibilities." The guys were fine emptying my bag—a result of their boyish nature. They'd find an empty bottle and a bush to park me behind and everything was fine. But there were places that simply weren't accessible, and though it sucked, I accepted the fact that I just couldn't go. In most circumstances, they bent over backwards to try to get me in.

I studied quite a bit more than I did in high school and became a pretty decent student, graduating as a member of the Class of 2016. I achieved this in four years, which is noteworthy, considering my disability, which often made college life more challenging than the norm. Thinking back to that day on the ice and recovering in the children's hospital, going to college hadn't even a seemed to be a possibility, let alone living independently and graduating in four years.

Each year, the graduating class donates a senior gift. Some classes donate scholarships, some plant trees, some construct memory benches. The class officers approached me and asked if they could create the Matt Brown Scholarship in my name. I accepted immediately and was both honored and humbled. In years prior, total donations reached around $15,000 for a scholarship. On graduation day, they announced that the scholarship bearing my name had tallied a school record of $70,000.

One Saturday, all the seniors gathered in the courtyard to party together one last time. Around midnight, everyone headed to the big house at top of the hill where the president's and admissions offices are located. The students and professors drank into the night together. It's a wonderful Stonehill tradition, and a great way to cap off four years of hard work and memories. We awoke the next morning and had to return to the very same spot to line up for graduation. It's so funny beginning at the graduation ceremony in the very location that had hosted the big drunk-a-thon only several hours before. The organizers strategically placed cases of water and even a few trash barrels around the area just in case. Everyone who attended could be seen wearing sunglasses to hide their bloodshot eyes.

The time for the graduation was now upon us. A ramp was set up at the side of the stage, and when I heard my name called, I made my way up the ramp and across the stage as the crowd cheered. This evolved into a standing ovation. I looked out at the crowd and had to bite my cheek to keep the tears back. It was the close of another chapter in my life; a chapter I never thought I would be a part of.

Now a couple years out of school, I am returning to Stonehill to get my master's. I have been hesitant to look for jobs because, since I graduated as an undergrad, I admit to having an unsubstantiated fear of failure. I feel that getting my master's will help me fine-tune the skills I learned as an undergrad, while helping me grow and understand the ever-changing aspects of marketing in the business world. I have a dream of helping a company soar to new heights or even running and sustaining my own company. When I was an undergrad, my dreams were simple: I wanted to prove my independence by living on campus, get out of my comfort zone, and make new friends. As I have gotten older, my dreams have changed. Just like before, my friends are moving into a new chapter of their lives, and it is time for me to move on as well.

CHAPTER 16

Two Words: Never Quit!

My mantra of "Never Quit" became imbedded in every fiber of my being while I was still at Boston Children's Hospital. Though I may wobble a bit from time to time in need of personal reassurance, I simply am not going to quit until I reach my goal. My goal is to take my recovery as far as medical science and technology will allow me to.

The motto came about when I was on the ride home from school with my aunt a few weeks before the MB3 Gala at The Garden. We discussed the slogan I needed for the apparel we were printing. I thought about my journey and what I was hoping to achieve in pushing daily towards my recovery. "Never quit," I confidently told her. We both loved it. It was simple and strong and assured. It expressed the confidence and commitment that I had possessed throughout my entire journey and the belief that I will carry with me until the day I step foot on the ground and walk again under my own power. I am honestly not certain how I define "full recovery," but whatever medical science, technology, hard work, grit, and determination will allow, I will NEVER QUIT until I experience it.

I try to relate this never-quit attitude whenever I speak to audiences. It doesn't matter what you're going through in life—whether it's something at work, at school, or with family, sports related or the largest obstacle one can ever imagine trying to conquer—quitting is never an option. You may stagger on occasion, you may question how you are going to proceed, but you can never allow yourself to stop pushing forward. Whenever you begin to doubt if the fight is worth the pain and effort, you need to lean on others around you for support. In return, you need to be ready to offer the same when people around you are in need.

We held our first MB3 Gala in 2010 at Gillette Stadium. I was still recovering in Atlanta at the time and couldn't experience the event firsthand. It was awesome to hear the incredible stories of financial and emotional support that stemmed from it. My parents say it was the greatest event they've ever witnessed. With wall-to-wall people attempting to enter the event, security was forced to control the crowd by letting in three people only when two had exited. Patriots coach Bill Belichick and team owner Robert Kraft were in attendance. People were coming up to the door without tickets solely to write checks. What the community did for me that night was a huge blessing, and it removed a tremendous weight from the shoulders of my family. It should be no secret that I suffered a very expensive injury, and what the town of Norwood and all of the supporters did for us that night was incredibly special.

The event was spearheaded by my uncle, Matt O'Neil. He advised that the first thing to be done following the injury was to fundraise like there was no tomorrow. "Otherwise," he said, "there would likely be no tomorrow." The organizers of the event wanted to do something really monumental, so they chose to hold the event at The Hall at Gillette Stadium. They held several planning sessions with the folks at Gillette, who assured us that they could handle an event of this size. Uncle Matt in turn advised them that whatever amount of Budweiser and Bud Light they normally had in stock should be doubled. "Norwood is going to drink every drop you have," he assured them. They said they had handled events like this before and had it covered. As Matt predicted, however, Norwood adopted my motto "Never Quit" and drank Gillette out of beer.

At the end of the night and with donations continuing to flood in following the event, over $750,000 was raised on my behalf. This was used for medical expenses, renovations of the house, medications, and anything that would be needed for my care. Through the fundraising, we have taken the financial strain off our family. Our fundraising goal is to not only cover all continuing care expenses but also to allow us to give to others who not have the tremendous support system that I have been lucky enough to have. We are in the process of filing paperwork to make the Matt Brown Foundation an official 501(c)(3) nonprofit, so we can continue to pay it forward and help others. Since the first gala at Gillette, we have done two additional events a year and a half apart to complete a trilogy of Boston's sports venues: one at TD Garden in September 2011 and one at Fenway in April of 2013.

As fundraising efforts took off, it became important that I learn to communicate my story. My first public speaking engagement took place about a year after I got hurt, when my younger cousin took me into her second-grade class for show-and-tell. As second graders I don't think they really cared about what I was going to say, but this represented my maiden voyage into the public-speaking arena. As we were walking in, my dad, aunt, and I were considering what types of questions the kids were going to ask me. I starting getting nervous in anticipation of what might come out of their innocent mouths. However, it was the complete opposite of what I anticipated. The first question was, "What's your favorite color?" The second inquiry, "What's your favorite food? Have you ever seen an R-rated movie? Do you like the month of June?" They were hysterical, firing off random questions for about twenty minutes straight. Not once was it, "How do you go to the bathroom?" Or, "How do you shower?" I think it helped ease my nerves for future speaking events, which I still get a bit apprehensive about, especially when preparing to speak to a more intimidating crowd.

A year later, I spoke in Sharon to a group about the same age. I finished sharing my story, and my aunt opened it up to the floor for questions. As is often the case, no one wanted to ask that first question. They just stared at me wide-eyed. Then, a boy in the second row raised his hand and asked a question I had never heard before. "If you could click a button and go back to the day you got hurt, would you do it?" Such a thoughtful question from the mind of an eight-year-old.

I didn't speak for several moments. I struggled mightily to answer. I had spent so much time working towards recovery that my injury had become part of who I was; I hadn't thought about reversing the past few years. I had unknowingly accepted my fate. I fumbled through my response and couldn't really muster up an intelligent answer. I took a few more softball questions and exited the room a bit flustered. Later on in the day, I thought about the question, and I have often pondered the response since. Believe it or not, I still struggle with the answer. Throughout this journey, I recognize that I have become a better person. I have matured more quickly than I would have had I picked up the puck cleanly and cleared it down the ice. I have met some of the most amazing people and become close friends with so many of them. I would have likely never been afforded the opportunity to experience so many amazing things had I deftly stepped aside from Tyler and raced down the ice with the puck stuck to my stick. The memories I've made will remain with me forever, and to lose all of that would weigh heavily on me. Ultimately, however, the answer to the question would be have to be yes: I would turn back the clock because losing the ability to walk and hold, to touch and feel, and to lift and hug are too large a price to pay for the wonderful experiences I've enjoyed.

When I got to college, I started speaking to other colleges and before bigger and older audiences. My first major speaking engagement was at Walpole High. It was at a South Shore Leadership Conference for high school students. This was my first time really speaking in front of an adult group, and I struggled. I had a major case of nerves, and I tried to go off my head rather than preparing my talk. As I shared stories and reminisced about the past and about Boston Children's and Atlanta, my mind got flooded with thoughts. I froze up on stage. My dad was there, and though he would never admit it, he knew how bad I was. A similar case of stage fright occurred at Pembroke High before I conquered my nerves and lack of preparation at Mansfield High. Though no one knew my story as well as I did, I learned that writing it down made it so much easier to revisit. I continued in this manner and have gotten much better since my rocky start. I love sharing my story and trying to instill the lessons that I've learned as a result of my injury, my rehab, my recovery and my never-quit mindset.

In addition to public speaking and the formation of the Matt Brown Foundation, I have also become an avid runner. I know what you're thinking. How can a man paralyzed from the neck down participate in the sport of running? I got involved in the sport through Dick and Rick Hoyt, Massachusetts locals who have competed in over 1,100 athletic events, despite the fact that Rick is in a wheelchair. Through them I learned that the sport of assisted running has become extremely popular.

Rick was born a quadriplegic with spastic cerebral palsy and is pushed by his now nearly eighty-year-old dad, Dick. Though the two don't run marathons or compete in full 140.6-mile triathlons together anymore, it is through their efforts that guys like me can participate in the Boston Marathon and other assisted events.

My running partner, Lucas Carr, and I were apparently destined to connect as far back as the early 2000s. Luke had dropped out of high school and started a tree-surgery business back in 1994. My grandparents needed some trees cut, so they hired Luke. Their house was situated near us, so my dad and I watched from our back window and witnessed this man climbing up the trees like a squirrel. Luke, a chainsaw hanging off his back, proceeded to cut down branch after branch with skill and ease. My dad and I marveled at the agility and the passion that he brought to his craft. We didn't actually meet Luke that day, but it didn't escape me how absolutely crazy he appeared to be.

Following my injury, while still at Boston Children's, Luke made it his responsibility as a citizen of the area to come meet me. He seemed to enter the room like the Tasmanian Devil cartoon character and has not spun out of our lives since. He visited me in Atlanta a few times and became extremely close with our family. One night while visiting our house, he causally asked me if I like to run. In true Lucas style, before I even had a chance to respond, we were taking my dimensions for a racing chair and had signed up for the Hyannis Marathon. Lucas doesn't do anything half way, so rather than starting with a five- or ten-kilometer race, we decided to start with a 26.2-mile jaunt around Hyannis, with aspirations of qualifying for the 2012 Boston Marathon.

The first time we ran together was just around the track up at the high school. It was really special and felt like I was running too. I hated running before my injury. Sprints at the end of practice were the absolute worst. As a quadriplegic, however, there is something liberating and free about feeling the wind in my face as we're racing around the track without me doing much of the physical work. Though I'm not running physically it takes a lot out of me. My heart rate increases, bouncing around in the chair takes a toll, and even trying to hold myself up and brace myself for any bumps is a physical strain on my body. It may not be quite as taxing as it is for Lucas, but I am very tired at the completion of most events. It's a good kind of tired, though, because I am out there competing while spreading the message of inclusion and "never quit" to those with disabilities.

Running through the streets of Hyannis was incredible. People yelled at us to "Keep it up! You're nearly there!" during the entire race. It was encouraging when we were at mile twenty-two, but not quite as much at mile one, when it was pretty clear that we were not "nearly there" and they were filling us with a sense of false hope. The best part of any marathon is the 26.2 miles of people screaming your name. Where else can you get a standing ovation for over four hours?

The weather was extremely cold, and since the course was a half-marathon loop we had to do it twice. We ran along the water and then had to turn around and do it again. It felt like the wind was in our face in both directions, and I was pretty chapped and wind burnt as we crossed the finish line. That race was a struggle, but Luke powered through it, and we were admitted into the Boston Marathon. Boston is different than other races in that you have to qualify by completing another marathon in under a certain time. We had succeeded in completing Hyannis in under five hours as a duo team.

As incredible as Hyannis was, competing in the Boston Marathon was surreal. Because the race is held in April every year, on Patriots Day, you're never quite sure what kind of weather you're going to get. In April of 2012, the first year we competed, the temperature was 95°F. Seasoned and novice runners alike were dropping like flies due to dehydration, but there was Lucas pushing not only himself but pushing me for the entire 26.2 miles. At noon, during the race, we climbed Heartbreak Hill with the sun right above us. Many houses had their sprinklers and hoses pointed towards the street so that runners could jog through the spray to cool down. I asked Luke several times if we should call it a day, concerned about his safety, but I knew in my heart of hearts that he could do it and would, of course, "Never Quit." Luke, an army ranger and army pathfinder who had served two tours of duty to Afghanistan, didn't have the word quit in his vocabulary. We finished right around 2:30 p.m. with a respectable time of 4:59:59. We crossed the finish line and headed right home. I took a cold shower and got into bed, but I didn't cool down until almost 10:00 p.m.

One of the highlights of anyone's Boston Marathon experience is running through Wellesley College. Wellesley College is an all-female private school located on Route 135 at mile 12.4 of the marathon route. The school is notorious for the "Scream Tunnel," where athletes are inspired and motivated for nearly a mile before the next 13.8 miles by the all-female chorus of cheers, which is nearly deafening. When you first hear the faint roar, about a mile away, it's not quite clear what the noise is. As you get closer, it gets louder and louder. The uneducated Boston Marathon athlete is still likely unclear what on earth they are hearing. Then it hits you like a wall of sound. The girls are hanging over the barriers, screaming, cheering you on, and holding signs that urge you to kiss them, marry them, and everything in between. I felt my heart beating through my chest as my adrenaline blew through the roof. It really gave Lucas, me, and many of the other 25,000 runners a boost to push for the last dozen or so miles.

There was something magical about running down Boylston Street towards the finish line in the most famous marathon of them all. It was my first time experiencing it and something I will never forget. The view is something out of a movie scene, and it seems like you a running in slow motion. I saw the finish line a couple hundred yards ahead and have a clear memory of every face in the crowd cheering us on as we ran the final .2 of the 26.2-mile race. As I looked around at the other runners, I witnessed a variety of unforgettable facial expressions as runners clawed their way to the finish line. At the five-hour finishing time, these are not the elite athletes who finished nearly three hours earlier. These are the regular Joes like me running the race of their lives in excruciatingly difficult conditions all to prove to themselves that they too possess a never-quit mentality. Some are smiling, some look like they're about to expire. That year, 2012, people were really struggling to get to the finish. There were people literally crawling to the finish line, simply refusing to give up on their goal of completing what they had started. I saw a young lady picked up and carried across the finish line by a complete stranger. In many ways, running and finishing the Boston Marathon is a metaphor for what I have been through since waking up in Boston Children's Hospital and my continued quest to walk again. I set a goal, I work tirelessly towards that goal, and I refuse to give up until I break the tape.

At this point in my recovery, I may still be struggling up Heartbreak Hill. Maybe I'm at Kenmore Square. I may even be onto Boylston Street with the finish line in sight. Because I don't know how far I have to go, I wake up every day and continue to work: the finish line may actually be closer than I think. I'm confident that a medical breakthrough is just beyond the horizon, so giving up this far into the race is not an option. Even if I have to crawl to the finish line to get there, I will get there.

As Luke and I approached the finish line, I looked forward to running by people I knew who were up in the grandstands cheering us on. It was incredible seeing the look of pride on the face of my family and friends. The past several years had been a marathon for Mom, Dad, Kelley, and Meghan, and I sense that they also felt they had accomplished something in seeing me cross the line. I completed something that I never would have done, injury or no injury. Before I met Luke, I had no interest in putting my body through that kind of torture, let alone as a quadriplegic. When I lay in bed at Boston Children's and thought about what was ahead in my future, running the Boston Marathon would have been laughable. Today, the medal stating "2012 Boston Marathon Finisher" hangs proudly in my room.

The following year, Luke and I intended to run it together again. But I had been sick that spring, and my doctors suggested I take the year off as it would not be good to put myself through the rigors of the event so soon after being ill. Luke contemplated whether or not to run without me. Both his girlfriend Erin and I urged him to experience the marathon solo. This was the year of the Boston Marathon bombing, and Luke finished a mere forty-five seconds before the first bomb went off. He crossed just in front of sidewalk where the initial explosion took place less than a minute later. Luke met Erin just beyond the finish line and had yet to receive his finishing medal. He heard the first explosion followed by the second, several seconds later. Being a veteran, he knew immediately what it was. Lucas told Erin where to meet him, and instead of running away, he turned and ran back into the war zone, and you can see him tirelessly tying tourniquets in the aftermath footage. That's just who Lucas Carr is. He would give you the shirt off his back in an ice storm. It makes me so happy to have someone like him care for me as much as he does. I'm also grateful that I was unable to participate that year. Had I participated, it's possible that Lucas and I, being a bit slower, would have found ourselves with another personal tragedy to deal with. I'm not certain that the Brown family could have survived another near miss or loss.

We decided to run the year after as part of the 2014 Boston Strong Marathon and the day was absolutely perfect. God could not have created a better day, and it was so appreciated following such a despicable event the year before. It was perfectly overcast, with rays of sun shining through, and a temperature of 60–65°F with a nice tailwind. I firmly believe that it was Martin Richard, Krystle Campbell, Lingzi Lu, and Officer Sean Collier looking down upon the masses to ensure that the day was flawless. I usually run with headphones on for a portion of the race to get lost in music while taking in the sites along the run. That day, wearing headphones didn't even enter my mind. The spirit of the Boston people was so incredible that I chose to soak up every sight, every sound, and every moment of this incredibly historic experience. I teared up a bunch that day. Taking the corner and running down Boylston Street was extremely emotional for runners and fans alike. I couldn't believe how large the crowd was that year, all the way from Natick and Ashland to the finish. The closer you got to Boston the deeper the crowd got. It swelled to nearly three of four deep on both sides of the road. Boston was just a mad house. Luke was feeling it that day and ran it in 3:30:00—an hour and a half faster than we did it in 2012. He was a man on a mission and was committed to crushing it.

In 2015, the weather was 45°F and rainy. It was so cold that I was chilled to the bone. This race was second only to 2018's for poor weather. Luke and I have run in all the elements and have grown to love each experience in its own special way, although 2015 was miserably hard. We skipped 2016, as I got an infection my leg and was in the hospital for ten days. Like anything, that too has become part of my marathon experience. Whether I am able to compete or need to view from the sidelines, the Boston Marathon has now become part of who I am. Pre-accident? Not a chance. Post-accident? I wouldn't miss it, whether I'm there physically or simply in spirit.

Following the marathon bombing in 2013, the city of Boston was rewarded with the Boston Bruins second trip to the Stanley Cup Finals in a three-year span. After beating the Canucks in 2011 for the first B's Stanley Cup in nearly forty years, we faced Chicago in the 2013 finals. Though we lost to the Blackhawks, I found myself in the middle of Boston Bruins lore.

During the playoff run, an army ranger jacket was presented by B's teammates to the Bruins player of the game. The Bruins have had a relationship with the rangers for several years and wore the army ranger T-shirt during the 2011 Stanley Cup run. Lucas, who is close friends with then Bruins defenseman Andrew Ference, helped fulfill Ference's wish of visiting a ranger base in Georgia following the 2011 Stanley Cup victory. Ference got to learn about the rangers and meet some of the guys. At the conclusion of his visit, they presented a jacket to Ference all patched up. Andrew once told me that most important thing on the jacket is the ranger patch because they go through hell to earn that. Andrew and the team didn't equate themselves to being rangers, but the jacket gave the team something to rally around while at the same time recognizing the rangers for what they do.

Following the team's loss to the Blackhawks, Andrew was about to head up to Edmonton. He stopped by my house to say goodbye to me. Andy walked into the house and had a bag with him. He came into my room, and we exchanged a few words before he pulled the jacket out of the bag and presented it to me. My jaw fell into my lap. I couldn't believe it. I said, "Are you kidding me? Do you know who wore this jacket? Do you know what the hell this thing is been through?" He said, "Yeah, but I need someone to look after it, and I think that should be you. You represent everything this jacket represents. Blood and guts, hard work, and glory." I had never been so honored. The guys at school absolutely loved it. The first time I asked the guys if they wanted to throw it on, they just stood there wide-eyed before taking pictures in it and sending it off to their friends.

CHAPTER 17

Stronger Together

By Kelley Brown

I was not at the game when Matt was hurt, though I had been to every game of the season. Hockey games were a big deal at our school, and our student section was always packed. I had been asked to go see a dance show followed by dinner with the girls from my dance studio and decided to go with them instead of going to this game. I'm not sure if that was a good thing or not. It was really just how things played out.

While I was at the dinner, Mom sent me a brief text saying that Matt had been hurt during his hockey game and they were going to the hospital. Matt had a history of injuries during sports from breaking his elbow during football, to multiple concussions, to others too many to recall. I just assumed that it was another injury of that sort and calmly told her to keep me updated. After dinner, I decided to go to one of the girls' house and hang out for a while. She was a friend I had known since I was five years old, so I was very close with her family. When we arrived at her house her mom was waiting outside for me. She advised me that she was going to take me home because my mom wanted me to feed our dogs. I considered that to be odd because I knew the dogs could wait a few hours to eat. This was when I started to realize there was more going on than what I was being told.

After going home and feeding the dogs, Mom told me to walk up to Gram's house. Gram had been diagnosed with cancer three months earlier and was starting to get really sick. Again, I was trying to piece things together at this point, so I assumed that my mom just didn't want her to be alone. As I was walking around the corner, I saw she was in the doorway waiting for me, and this is when my heart really sank. She had been so sick that she rarely got up, and I knew if she had the strength to wait for me, something was up. While still standing in the middle of the street, one of Matt's best friends, Amy Moynihan, called me and explained what was going on. The Moynihans were our old neighbors and life-long family friends, so Mom had reached out to Amy's mom to ask her to call me.

I didn't hear from my parents for a long time that night because they were understandably preoccupied. I eventually started to receive short updates via text from my mom, but they were all very vague. Eventually, she told me that my dad would be home in the morning to bring me in to see Matt. My two cousins, Callie and Abby, came over to Gram's house and said they would sleep over with me that night. We stayed up all night talking about what we thought was going to happen. We had few details about the situation, so our conversations were mainly speculating that Matt would be home in a few days, maybe a week, and was going to be okay. We just stayed positive about the situation.

I created the Facebook group "PRAY FOR MATT BROWN #3" that night, still not knowing the extent of Matt's injury but thinking it would be a nice group to allow Norwood friends to remain positive. In the eight years the group has grown to over 38,000 followers. I never expected that, but it continues to be a great way for our family to give updates on Matt's journey.

When Dad picked me up the next morning, he could barely speak. He said that my mom would talk to me when we got there, and the rest of the ride was silent. I have driven up and down the coast many times between Boston and North Carolina, and I still think that drive to the hospital was the longest of my life. It was also the first time I had ever seen Dad cry.

Going to school the next day was extremely overwhelming. I pushed myself to go back, but I couldn't stay the whole day. The attention was just too much for me. I felt like a celebrity, for lack of a better word, but in the worst way possible. Everyone asked for information, bombarded me with hugs, and checked in to see how I was. Some just stared at me unsure of what to even say. I was only fourteen at the time but have come to understand that this is a natural reaction. I am extremely appreciative of how much everyone cared. My dean, Jim Forrest, became a savior to me. He would let me come to his office whenever I felt overwhelmed or couldn't focus, and he would make sure I was getting my school work done (I came in late or left school early with regularity following Matt's accident). School became one of my biggest struggles after Matt was hurt. I had always been a good student prior, but my attendance began to suffer.

During my sophomore year, Matt returned to school. It felt like we had just begun to adjust to our "new life" and then his return to school added a whole new chapter of adjustment. I tried to accept the fact that every situation that presented itself would end up just fine, and I would eventually learn to cope better. Instead, I became very angry at our situation and wondered why it was happening to us. I had a hard time coping and just wanted things to be the way they used to be. My school work suffered, and I earned some of the worst grades of my life. I had a small bump in the road during that period, and I felt like giving up. Thankfully, by junior year, I was able to get back on track, things normalized a bit, and my grades improved.

A few days after Matt's injury, there was a large church service held to offer prayers for Matt. It was just Dad and me at home that day, and he was still having a really hard time. It was held very early, before school, so that everyone who wanted to go could attend, and it was packed. Dad and I snuck in, keeping our heads down, and sat near the back. We thought that if we were seen, everyone would want to see how we were doing, which I don't think we wanted at the time. Though extremely appreciative of everyone caring so much, it was still very new to us, and I'm not sure we were ready to talk about it. The service was beautiful, and Dad took me out to breakfast afterwards. One of the only faces I knew at the church was our principal, also a family friend, George Usevich. He became very involved in Matt's journey and played a huge role in making sure Matt's high school experience went as smoothly as possible.

Prior to the game following Matt's injury, I called Mom to ask if I could wear Matt's jersey that night. She was concerned because she knew there was going to be a lot of press there, but I was young, so I really didn't understand why. She had told me I could wear the now-famous "3" jersey, but I had to stay with two of her best friends, Nancy Mahon and Anne Marie Cathcart, who are mothers of two of Matt's best friends and teammates. She was worried that the press was going to bombard me with questions and camera lenses, and was she right! It was miserable trying to even get into the game, but I did what Mom advised and stayed close to Mrs. Mahon and Mrs. Cathcart.

During the game, Chris O'Brien, a senior on the team, was checked hard into the boards and was unable to get up after falling to the ice. It was an all-too-familiar scene for Norwood. He was wheeled off the ice by paramedics, and we were told he was also going to be taken to Boston Children's Hospital where Matt was staying. I texted my mom, and her first response was "No way," followed by "Because that's not funny!" I was unable to respond to Mom because the press had surrounded me to ask questions about how I felt about Chris's injury. I couldn't answer as I was having a difficult time wrapping my head around Matt's injury, let alone another one. I was quickly escorted out of the rink to protect me from the swarm of reporters and photographers. Chris was one of my good friends, and I really couldn't imagine that the same thing had happened to him. Once they removed me from the rink, Mrs. Cathcart called my mom to explain the situation. Mom was able to visit Chris in the hospital that night, and thankfully he was okay.

I tend to cope with things in a much different manner than many people, and in Matt's case, I became very angry about what occurred rather than sad. I did not cry at all but instead searched to find ways to get my anger out. I'd often ask myself why I wasn't crying and felt like I was a bad person for my lack of emotion. It was a long time before reality set in. About a year after he had gotten hurt, I was upstairs in my room, and he yelled up to me to come down quick. I rushed down thinking something serious may have happened. He asked me if I could scratch his nose for him and told me it is the most frustrating thing to have an itch that you can't scratch. This was the moment I was finally able to put myself in his shoes and understand what he was going through. Reality hit me like a brick. I ran upstairs and cried for hours. All of my bottled-up emotions poured out. I only told Matt this story recently. I didn't understand at the time what a monumental moment it was for me.

When Matt graduated college, I felt extremely proud to call him my brother. When he first became paralyzed, the idea of going to and graduating from college was crossed off the list of accomplishable goals. But with support and determination to make it happen, he was able to live away from home for all four years and have the same college experience that most high school seniors dream about. It became another valiant effort to change the stigma surrounding spinal injury. The fact that he still managed to graduate in less time than I did is something I don't really care to talk about! His graduation day was more than just receiving a college diploma. I often tease Matt that with his high school study habits, it would have shocked us all if he had graduated even without the injury. In truth however, it represented how far he had come since being injured, and how he was never going to let his injury define him or keep him from following his dreams.

Every now and then I need to remind myself of how well we have all adjusted as a family. We will continue to improve even more over time. Though his graduation was the pinnacle for Matt in my eyes,

I'm very proud of him every single day. He has become the example of how being paralyzed doesn't have to ruin your life. He is fighting each day for a better life for those with spinal cord injuries, and is working tirelessly to change the statistics of recovery.

Since Matt's accident, I accept the fact that my relationship with my parents has changed. They care for me no less than they care for Matt but in a different way than they had before. Through the outstanding amount of love and support they have provided for me over the years, they have shown me how much they care for me. I will forever be indebted to them. I no longer have one ounce of anger about how the dynamic in my household changed. It has helped me to grow into the strong, independent, hardworking, and grateful woman that I am today, and though I wish I had my former annoying older brother back, two things will never change: Matt will always remain older and will always be annoying.

Matt's injury had a huge impact on my future vocation, and for that I'll be forever grateful. When I was ten years old, I was diagnosed with a rare auto-immune disorder called chronic recurrent multifocal osteomyelitis. CRMO caused me to become very sick and in extreme pain for many years as a child. During this time in my life, I was the major focus of my parents. I was constantly in and out of the hospital, and it consumed a lot of my parents' time. I wanted to be just like all of the nurses that cared for me. When Matt was hurt, the frequency of being in and out of hospitals obviously increased immensely, and during that time I fell in love with the pediatric ICU. I loved the fast pace, and though surrounded by chaos, everyone had this way of remaining calm. I admired how smart they all were and the difference they made to not only my brother's life but also the lives of entire families. I knew that's what I wanted to do, too.

Before Matt's injury, I had always believed that I would stay relatively close to home for college. After the injury, it felt like moving away would allow me to escape the constant reminders of what had happened. I went through a phase of feeling like I had lost my identity.

I was referred to as "Matt's sister" and never by just Kelley. No one intended to do it, and I feel the need to stress how proud I am to be Matt's sister, but to be quite frank, it really bothered me. That's when I made the decision to apply to colleges far away from home. It was never to try and get away from what was going on at home; it was only a way for me to find myself. Ironically, one of my very first nights at college, I was hanging out with some people I had just met, and someone asked me where I was from. When I responded that I was from a small town outside of Boston, their first response was, "Do you know Matt Brown?" The guy who asked was from Rhode Island and had gone to a concert and met Matt two weeks before coming back down to school. All I could do was laugh. It reminded me quickly of how much I love my family and where I am from, but that this was the change that I needed.

I was still in the prime of my sickness when Matt got hurt, so it was a huge adjustment for me. It was difficult because there were times I really needed my parents to tend to me as they always had. I never told them because I didn't want to add anything else to their plate. I can confidently say that I have never felt any anger towards my parents; my anger was about the circumstances themselves. I have gone through feelings of frustration, but this is no different than the feelings Matt and my parents have experienced as well. Matt's accident caused me to grow up a lot faster than kids my age usually do. I became frustrated because I didn't want to deal with some of the things other kids my age may never endure during their lifetimes, but the more independent I became, the less my parents had to worry about.

I am now twenty-two and working as a full-time registered nurse at my dream job in the neonatal ICU. I live alone and manage my life completely on my own. I look back on having to grow up faster than my friends, and I am thankful for it. I wouldn't be who I am today without facing the hardships that we had to endure. Despite everything, my parents have taught me how to persevere and to come out on top. Overall, I think we've done the best we can to handle the situation. But the life lessons I have learned, and how much I've grown through this journey, outweigh any of the obstacles we've had to overcome.

I had a lot more exposure to certain skills and situations than others in my nursing class due to being stand-in caretaker for my brother. During my first semester, I had a patient that was in a car accident and was paralyzed. Many students in my clinical cohort were afraid to work with him because they weren't sure how to handle the situation. I was lucky enough to use the knowledge I had learned from Matt while providing care to this patient. During nursing school, I learned that you can teach almost anyone the skills to become a nurse, but you can't teach people ethics or how to develop relationships with patients. Matt had a few nurses who really stood out because of the relationship they were able to form with him and our family. From those experiences, I learned how I wanted to be as a nurse and the type of relationships I wanted to form with my patients and families. This is a skill not everyone possesses because they were never on the receiving end of good care.

I've always been extremely thankful for my parents. I am lucky enough to have two amazing people in my life to admire and look up to. My relationship with my parents has only grown stronger since Matt's accident. They were open with me when things got tough, which allowed me to help in whichever way I could. Our relationship transitioned from a parent-daughter relationship into one of friendship. I can't express enough my love and admiration for my parents. They have shown me what strength truly is and exemplified that true love can get you through. Our family leans on each other for support, and everyone has specific roles in the dynamic. We have developed a way of functioning, and I think everyone has played a part in keeping this journey positive. In a fantasy world, if given the option to be part of a different family, I wouldn't trade mine for the world. They have shaped who I am today.

My relationship with Matt has grown stronger than I would

have ever imagined. I know that the bond we have formed will never change. I plan on moving home to the Norwood area at some point and buying a house that we can both live in together. I think it would be a wonderful experience for the both of us if the opportunity arises. Matt is one of the most important people in my life, and I know many of my life decisions over the next few years will be driven by what he needs from me. I know he would never ask me to change my life solely to help him, but it's something I will do if necessary. He's always been someone I can lean on, and both of us will make life decisions while keeping the other in mind. I'm excited to see what the future has in store for both of us. Life may never get easier, but we sure have gotten stronger together as a result of it.

CHAPTER 18

Wisdom Accepted by a Really Proud Dad

By Mike Brown

Matt played hockey for as long as I can remember, so when I think about Matt's life, even prior to the accident, the game of hockey is intertwined deeply into my thoughts about him. Being the parent of a young hockey player was a wonderful experience. I had played sports during my youth, all through high school and even into college, but I had never played ice hockey. My wife's side of the family was the hockey side. My side of the Brown gene pool contributed the baseball, basketball, and football acumen.

Some of my siblings knew how to skate, and though I wasn't much of a skater, I absolutely loved the sport. I tried skating a few times growing up since we lived beside a pond, but I was never really good at it. I always ended up as the kid in net with the green boots whining at the other kids not to lift the puck or else it's a penalty. I had friends in the neighborhood who played hockey, and I always tagged along with their parents to watch them play. In high school, I was friendly with the hockey team, and in college I would never miss a game. Growing up, I obviously watched the Bruins, being lucky enough to watch Bobby Orr. And Eddie Westfall was guest speaker at our Little League banquet.

As Matt got older and started to get into the game more, I enjoyed taking him to the rink for games and practices and being a part of it.

It was a highlight watching him skating with his friends. Parenting a hockey kid is an amazing commitment, as it was not just for the Brown family, but for the hundreds of thousands of families across the United States, Canada, and the world. Driving all over to skate at ridiculously odd hours, leaving the house at 5:00 a.m. with your kid asleep in the back seat, going down to the Cape, north to New Hampshire, or if you're lucky to the town next door. It became part of who we were and what we did as a family. Next thing you know, you're heading to tournaments in Lake Placid or Maine or back down to the Cape.

There's a camaraderie amongst the parents that forms standing in the cold rink early in the morning. Someone makes a run to Dunkin' Donuts to make sure everyone has their coffee. A connection builds between dads and moms like in no other sport. You see that even at the pro level: if you play the game, you are connected for life, part of the fraternity, and parents share the same connection. It's a big commitment, but I believe it's a commitment that every parent loves to make and looks back on with the realization that we had a great time.

Youth hockey is different than Little League. Kids play tournaments all the time and do a lot traveling together as youth hockey players. Maybe the magic formula for why players are the way they are is that they remember where they came from; whether junior or pro, you see it at all levels. The teams even have travel-with-dad or travel-with-mom road trips. You head out with four kids, four dads, and four hockey bags during an overnight trip in a rented van. The closeness of the hockey parents might also be due to the conditions. Playing the game in the dead of winter, it's dark and cold, causing parents and fans to stand closer together to watch their kids play. In baseball you're out in right field in a lawn chair, while some other dad is on the third base side in the bleachers.

A hockey player and their family seem grounded and humble and don't ever forget their roots. No NHL player forgets Mom and Dad getting him up early, getting him to practice, getting him into the locker room early, getting him dressed, tying his skates, getting him on the ice, patting him on the back.

As a father, you try to raise a son that is honest, upright, and polite. Someone who is going to grow up to be a nice young man, a nice adult. Sports help a young boy (or girl) to meet other kids and get out and run around. When Matt was younger, we signed him up for a bunch of sports to see which he gravitated to. We started with baseball, soccer, and hockey just to give him the opportunity to experience each. One of my friends reached out and said, "We need another player on the hockey team. Why don't you bring Matt over?" I responded, "Listen, Dave. Matt's only been skating for about six months. I don't know if he's ready." Dave assured me that they don't look for talent at this level. "We typically look for good kids with good parents and Matt fills the bill."

As a father, you guide your kids and just try to be a good parent. You teach them important things along the way, like how to throw or kick a ball and how to make them strong and confident, so they can start doing things on their own. Kindergarten is the first time they stop clinging to your leg, and when you say, "I'll see you in a couple hours," they stand up straight, give you a wave, then they're off. You know he's sick to his stomach, but as a father you recognize that he has a little juice and can do it. You see your son develop in big ways and small ways. You try to teach him the proper way to behave, even at that age, such as how to shake people's hands and look them in the eye. That was something my father taught me, and these are the foundation-builders that have helped Matt become such an amazing young man.

Before the accident, two friends whom I respect highly approached me to share their opinions on Matt. John is a plumber and Marty is a sheet rock guy who does ceilings and board. They are tough guys; family guys who raised a couple of sons and daughters of their own. I recall walking into the grocery store and spotting John. We stopped to talk for a few minutes, and as I started to walk away, he stopped me. "Hey, you know what I meant to tell you, Mike? That kid of yours, I love him. Every time I see him he asks me, 'Hey, Mr. O'Rourke. How's it going?' He shakes my hand and looks me straight in the eye. I love that kid." Matt was probably twelve or thirteen at the time, and it made me so proud. A couple years later, I ran into Marty O'Brien at one of Matt's baseball games. "Hey, Mike, before I forget, that kid of yours … dynamite. I see all of these piss ants roaming around, and I ask them 'Hey, what are you all doing?' They just turn their backs and shrug their shoulders. But, not your kid. He looks me square in the eyes, shakes my hand, and says, 'Hey, Mr. O'Brien.' You know, your kid is all right." Those are two guys who know right from wrong. They were raised right and raised their own kids right. To have them call out your kid at such a young age gave me such pride. My wife and I deserve credit, but we just laid the foundation. Matt has developed into his own man. You just put them on the right path, and then the decisions they make are their own.

After the injury, Matt had some major decisions to make. He had to start dealing with this thing that happened. He had to decide if he was going to fight it, or if he was going to stay positive or be pissed off, or whether to face it head-on or skirt around the issue. Those are tough decisions for a fifteen-year-old to make. But through his choices, he has taught us to stay positive. To watch him go out every day and navigate all the obstacles, and to see the profound impact he has on elementary school kids, is inspiring. His mission has become to dispel the notion that those in wheelchairs are not able by throwing on his lights and showing the kids what he can do.

This adoration of Matt extends to sportscasters, professionals, and many business professionals. They all nod and say, "My God" after speaking with him. Matt's attitudes about his disability comes from his heart, and he doesn't let it define who he is. I have learned so much from him by just being close to it, being his chauffeur, and watching how he navigates everything. He engages people, and you see a look on their face when he does it.

Whenever Matt would leave for a game, we'd wish him good luck. The last thing I would tell him was to keep his head up. That could have come from watching Travis Roy get hurt. This game is quick; you get hit, bang, you get up, and you go. It was an exciting game. Keeping your head up is something that is inherent in hockey players. The night of Matt's injury, I went down to the game with my older brother Brian and a few guys from Lewis's—a local bar in town. Typically, I would stand with the other parents, but that night I was down the far end of the rink during the first period. I saw some dads I knew gathering at the other end, so I decided to stand with them for the second period. My wife Sue had gotten to the game by then, so just by happenstance, I ended up standing next to her. This never happens during games, as she's normally with the moms and I'm with the dads. That night, we were standing side-by-side next to each other right where Matt hit. He literally hit at our feet.

Initially, I thought he just got his bell rung or maybe a concussion. He ended up on his side, and we made eye contact. He had a look of fear, and his eyes were darting back and forth. His body was still as he lay on his right side looking up. I yelled to him "Are you okay?" Carl Cathcart, who was next to me, said, "Oh boy, he hit hard." I moved down the glass trying to get a closer look. I was thinking maybe he got knocked out or broke his collarbone. I knew it was more serious when the refs came over and called for assistance. My wife tried to get onto the ice, and the referee was holding her back before realizing that she was the mother. I don't even know how many minutes passed, but by the time the EMT got there, Anne Cathcart, an emergency room nurse, was already on the ice. Anne was talking to him when we finally got on the ice. He said to me, "Dad, I can't feel anything." I looked at his face and said, "It's going to be okay. Stay still." I put my hand under his jersey on his hip and rubbed it asking if he could feel it. He said, "I think so, maybe. No I can't." I then started pinching him and asked if he could feel it. Again, he said no.

Anne called over to Brendan. Brendan is her son and one of Matt's best friends. He skated over and he and Matt exchanged some words. Brendan started to cry, so his mom kicked him out saying, "If you're not going to help, get out of here."

Sue and I stood there and watched it all play out. You could hear a pin drop. Time started to move so slowly. I never once thought he could have broken his neck and be paralyzed. I thought it was maybe a stinger or shock. They got him on the backboard, and Sue went with him in the ambulance. I jumped in my car and followed the ambulance over to South Shore Hospital. We got to the ER and started to talk with the doctors. They allowed us to go see where they put him, and it was here that I realized it's serious.

I could hear Matt talking and flirting with one of the young nurses. Sue and I were observing it all. Then his left hand, which was draped across his chest, slipped and fell off the table. His arm looked like a belt hanging in a closet. It was limp and there was no muscle to it. I turned my back to the table he was lying on and started to cry. That's the moment it hit me. I said, "Holy shit, this is serious. He is hurt bad." Sue turned to me, grabbed my arm and said, "You need to get it together. You can't do this in front of him."

They took him in to do the X-rays and CAT scan, and that's when we first saw the vertebrae. The doctors called us over and showed us. It almost looked like someone took a chisel with a cross on it and hit both of those vertebrae, splitting them into four pieces. There were no fragments or shards. It was a clean break.

The doctors said they were going to transfer him to Boston Children's Hospital because he was showing signs of paralysis from the injury. They didn't know if it was permanent or temporary but let us know it was serious and they need to get him to where they had experts.

Matt went into the ambulance with Sue. I went to the waiting room, and there were a bunch of Norwood parents there. One of my friends, Dave Glaser, offered to drive me to Boston Children's while another drove my car behind us. I think they were worried about me driving. I talked to Dave on the way in and said, "Holy shit, this is a nightmare. I want to wake up from it. How did this happen?" Dave listened and said all the right things to quell my anxiety.

We arrived two minutes after the ambulance, and the staff got Matt into the emergency room. There was already a team working on him. He had vomited at South Shore, and they had to roll him. They were stabilizing him and doing assessments while talking to Sue and me. They took him for more X-rays and CT scans. They gave him meds to keep him stable, now that they confirmed they were dealing with a spinal cord injury. Despite all the activity, I felt like everyone was moving in slow motion.

With my father being a physician and taking care of so many people, we started to see a lot of people we knew. My sister, Nancy, made her way in to the hospital and joined us in the waiting area. She and her husband, David, were in town on a gift that my wife and I had given to them. They were actually in the waterfront area, and my brother Brian told them that Matt got hurt. Nancy is a nurse, and she let us know she would be there if we needed anything. She was sending positive thoughts.

Matt was wheeled up to Seven South, the ICU floor, and was surrounded by every machine known to man. They showed Sue and me the CAT scans, MRIs, and X-rays, and we could see the gray around his cord. They told us he was paralyzed but they won't know for forty-eight hours if was just shock to the spinal cord or something more long term.

Staying in his room that night and watching Sue holding his hand, my mind was focused on him. Matt, my son. I was just really trying to wrap my head around everything. Did this actually happen? Sue and I were in the room together for the first three days before realizing that one of us could stay while the other headed home to try getting some rest, get some things done, grab some stuff, and then trade off every day.

I came home that first night and was going to sleep in our bed.

I sat down on the edge of the bed and had myself a good cry again. It was one of those good cries, releasing everything you had held inside, like when you were eight years old and your first dog died. It was a gut-wrenching sorrow. I didn't cry for me. It was for Matt. This kid was now in a fight for his life, facing paralysis. In just a few days he would be having neck surgery to stabilize everything, and I started to realize that it was for real. I don't think I could ever feel as sad as I did during the first week.

Once it settles in, you start to realize what lies ahead. There are a lot of decisions to be made in a very short amount of time. People are starting to talk about the long-term prognosis and where to go next. Where would he attend physical therapy? Spalding or the Shepherd Center? How could Sue and I juggle this as full-time employees?

After about four days, Matt started to come to. He still had his breathing tube in. He had difficulty communicating, so we devised the letter board game, pointing to letters and spelling words. We tried to talk to him and to keep him calm.

My wife had some amazing answers for him right off the bat that I never would have had. "I don't want to be paralyzed, Mom," he said. My wife said, "Nobody said you will be, Matt. So you focus on hope. It going to be a long road, but no one said you will never walk again, so let's not focus on that right now." It was as if Sue had rehearsed this before and knew exactly what to say.

The nurses come in every day to help babies fighting for their lives, to help kids and their families deal with sickness and death. I learned something important from one of the ICU nurses when I asked him how they did that work every day. The nurse said, "If I can get through my twelve-hour shift and everything is okay by the end of it, you know, it's been a good day. I go home and come back thinking about the next twelve-hour shift. I don't think about yesterday or tomorrow. I just think about today." I adopted the same belief, and it was life-altering. Is he stable right now? What decisions need to be made today? Being in the business and sales industry, looking ahead and forecasting is a big part of what we do, so switching my mindset by thinking only about today and not worrying about tomorrow or next week was different for me. It was therapeutic. Spending those first couple days in Boston Children's drove home the point about what was important. You're looking at your child in the hospital bed, paralyzed, and you start to think, *Who gives a shit about anything else? How could I worry about anything else other than making this kid okay?*

As all of this was happening, I thought about our daughter Kelley and what goes into trying to raise a daughter. We taught her many of the same things we taught Matt—how to be polite, behave well in front of others, be confident—and we introduced her to sports. She tried sports, but none was her cup of tea. Though she was fast and strong, she gravitated to dance. She became a very good dancer, and I was very proud of that. I watched her stand up in front of a crowd of 600 people at ten years old and introduce herself, "Hi my name is Kelley Brown. I am from K & M Dance Studio, and I am going to give an interpretive dance." She went out and did amazingly well, and although I'm not a big dance-recital guy, I went to all of them and was blown away with how well she did.

When Matt got hurt, Kell was just fourteen. She was coming into her own young adulthood and dealing with everything that girls go through entering high school. Then her brother ended up all over the news and in the paper, and it was very hard for her. In those immediate hours after you learn that your brother is hurt badly, it weighs on you. Everyone is asking about him, while no one is asking about you. It was really easy to pay attention to Matt at that time, but when one of our relatives said, "Hey, Kelley is really having a hard time," I pulled her aside and asked, "What's going on? What's happening?"

She said, "You just have to remember that you have another kid."

A lump formed in my throat upon hearing a fourteen-year-old educate me as a parent.

"I'm a part of this family. I'm going through this too."

I said, "You are right. You are a big part of it."

Kelley was a big part of it. She became Matt's scribe and his voice before he had one again. She sat with him and read all of his messages, going through his Facebook. She was our official media person.

I told her that she had a right to be angry and to be sad, but she shouldn't internalize it or hold it in, telling her, "You can't sit in the corner and sulk and kick and yell. Let us know what you're feeling so that we can help." She embraced it, and it's been wonderful to see how she has navigated everything with the media and the public appearances, going places with him as Matt Brown sister, and hearing people saying, "That's Matt Brown's sister." It takes a hell of a lot of grace and courage to accept the second-sibling role. She has done amazingly well, and it is amazing to see the young woman she has grown to be.

She went away to school, to get out from under the Matt Brown shadow. She ended up a thousand miles away in North Carolina. This was very hard to do. But she battled with some homesickness, pushed herself through a lot, but came out with a nursing degree and a job three days after graduating, which is extremely impressive and a tribute to her inner strength. She now works in the neonatal care unit in North Carolina and is an amazing person in her own right.

Kelley never forgets what she went through with Matt and what she learned from him, and he remembers what he learned from her. As siblings they were always pretty close. Matt is such a good kid that he never wanted to tell us when things were bothering him, so he would tell Kelley. She became a huge confidant to him. She really helped him through some problems and would give us a heads up only if needed, but would never compromise their mutual trust.

You look at your kids and think of how blessed you are. They are strong, confident, and polite. They know right from wrong, and are socially engaging. They can carry on a good conversation, which in this day and age is pretty cool. To see your kid engage in a conversation about life or society with an adult is meaningful. We did pretty well with Kelley as well, but again, she is a girl who created her own path. We just laid the foundation.

As a couple, Sue and I have braved a pretty intense storm. I reflect back to the first vacation we took following the injury, which was about three or four years later. We were constantly wondering if he was all right. Are the nurses and the aides doing what we would do? Matt has his routines, like anyone who was gone through an injury. They want stuff done the same way because I think it's a feeling of consistency and control. So, when a personal care assistant comes in, it may take them twenty-five minutes to do what I can do in ten, things like getting him into the shower. The vacation was warranted, but these are the things you think about instead of relaxing and taking a breath. When you are at home, there's no hiding from it. You are reminded of it every day by getting him up or into bed or showering him. The situation affects the entire family and how you look at life. It impacts personal plans, long-term plans, and business planning from both a functional and financial standpoint. Is he going to be paralyzed for five years, ten years, or even fifty years? How are we going to afford that and make sure he's comfortable? Suddenly, you stray from thinking day-to-day, and you start to broaden it. It changes your life plan. Plans that were once, "We will work until the kids will be off on their own and married. We will retire to Arizona. I will golf, while you will hang out with your sister," are all out the window. You don't think about those things anymore.

Going through a tragedy and a trauma, you meet other families that have gone through the same. You are now in that fraternity whether you like it or not. We have been lucky enough to meet some incredible people and families. We've met paraplegics and quadriplegics and an incredibly high number of families that have fallen apart. Many times you learn that a mother left or a father left. They didn't sign up for this or they can't handle it. There's a part of me that understands how people close the door, but this is reality. This is the hand you were dealt, so how are you going to play it? Sue and I agreed that although this is not we imagined, we were going to deal with this. Sue is a really, really strong lady, and we signed on for whatever came our way. She's been leading the way most of the time and making sure the family is good. Making sure Matt's good. It has been a conscious choice. We were close before, and this has made us closer. We share something that might have broken up other couples that weren't as close or strong. We have known each other a very long time and were raised by similar parents, strong people in their own right. It never goes away, but it's the new normal. Nevertheless, we still find ways to laugh and have a good time. It may take longer to get places, and there's anxiety watching his chair get loaded onto the plane and hoping it's in one piece when you get to your destination. There are everyday tasks that become much more work with someone in a wheelchair, but you learn to overcome and you learn to deal. "We'll figure it out" has become one of our most commonly used terms now.

Once you accept the changes you start to travel again. You start to fly to Las Vegas. You drive to Louisville or Florida. You start to live again. Matt has become fairly independent. He is okay staying home alone if his aide isn't there. Matt is fine solo, whether he is on his phone or laptop. Sue and I can go out to grab a bite to eat and bring him home something if he wants. You do realize, however, that he is a 24/7 dependent. Someone has to get him into bed and get him out. One of the first times I really realized that was when we dropped him off for college. At home, we became so comfortable leaving him "on his own" that we forget that you are really still only twenty feet from him. Then it comes slamming into us that he is completely dependent and someone is going to need to be with him in his room. Someone is going to need to come in and get him up and into bed. Someone's going to need to walk to class with him and be in class with him. He dealt with all that very well, which is an amazing thing in itself. You think of your kid being dropped off at college and how nervous they are, then imagine what Matt was going through being eighteen and a quadriplegic.

There are moments I remember so well. Moments like the first time we got to the Shepherd Center, going up to his room and watching them transfer him into his bed. They had two sip-and-puff straws, one for the TV, one to call the nurse. They showed Matt how to operate the straws, and then they left the room. I sat down in the chair next to the bed and the nurse came back in to remind me that parents were not allowed to stay overnight in the room. Matt would be in the room alone. They introduce independence into the minds of not only the kids but also the parents too. Mom and Dad won't always be there, so it's time to start trusting others. They shut off the lights, and I was sitting in the chair with only a few minutes to go before I had to leave. I remember clear as day what Matt said to me. He said, "You know what, Dad? I'm not going to look backward anymore. I'm not going to worry about why this happened or how it happened, I'm just focused on moving forward and working to beat this, and am going to focus on the future." I was impressed that this fifteen-year-old kid who just flew 1,500 miles to Georgia on a med flight, who got put in an ambulance and into a bed at this unfamiliar hospital, had the ability to say that he was not worried about the past and was just going to focus on the future.

I realized that was his decision. Not mine, not Sue's, but his decision. It was at that moment I knew he's going to be okay. This was a huge turning point, and he has never looked back. He faces it every day and tries to beat it every day. No matter how long it takes, he's never going to stop because why would you? We both share the same philosophy. Why would you ever stop when tomorrow could be the day? What if tomorrow is when a medical breakthrough happens? What if tomorrow his arm starts to wake up and his legs do the same? What if tomorrow is the day? Why would you ever stop?

Another incident I remember distinctly is when he finally got the tube out. He asked me, "Dad why did this happen? I don't want to be paralyzed."

I said, "Yeah, buddy, I know how you feel."

He stopped me right there. "Dad, you have no idea how I feel."

It was like I had someone kick me in my stomach.

"Don't kid yourself saying you know how I feel, Dad. I'm the one who's paralyzed," he said.

I swallowed hard and said to him, "You're right, I don't know, but I am here for you and will always be here for you, and I will be your biggest cheerleader. I won't make the mistake of knowing what it feels like."

Matt didn't say much after that, but he knew I got it, and I did get it. That day, we both grew as father and son, player and cheerleader, teacher and student.

Shepherd Center was a great place. They taught him how to get prepared to live in a wheelchair for however long that may be. They taught him how to navigate the world in the chair, and that was a really cool thing. They also showed Sue and me how to get him dressed, get him into the chair, and do all the really personal body care. Sue had a medical background, so for her it was second nature. For me, it was "Holy crap. I'm doing what?" Though my father was a physician, I had enough of a problem looking at my own blood, let alone someone else's. Yet it became second nature to me too, ultimately. It's amazing what you can do when you are doing it for your son, your daughter, or your wife. When we left the hospital with just a bag full of supplies and were on our own, it was kind of like bringing home a new born child for the first time.

We were constantly tired, and we are even still. That's just a given now. Matt has spasms in the middle of the night that we need to go down and fix, but you just get into the rhythm. On occasion, I go to North Carolina for a few days of golfing, and Sue goes out to a conference in Las Vegas. We both love going away together, but we have realized the importance of sending one another away for some rest and relaxation. When one of us goes away, we know that he's home with the other and going through the routine that he likes. When we both go away, he's got an assistant getting him up in the morning and nurses coming and going. It's not done the way he likes it, so it is always on your mind. I can send Sue away with girlfriends or her sisters, knowing it will give her some time to relax, and she does the same for me. Both of us are realists and understand that we need some me time because we have both worked for it. Everybody realizes that, whether it's Kelley or Matt's aide, Pat. You just can't do it 365 days a year, year after year, without burning out. You're no good if you're sick. We need to stay strong for him.

I am often asked if I believe in the theory that you are never given more than you can handle, and I don't know if I agree. I have seen people trying to shoulder an amount that has hurt them. That has broken them. That has crushed their spirits. Unfortunately, you see folks that are overwhelmed, and though everyone is trying to help them, they just can't emotionally handle any more. What I think you are given and how you handle it relies on a couple of factors. The first is you: how do *you* handle it? The second is your support system and how the people in it help you understand you are not going through this alone. You begin to realize that there people around you, picking up the pieces, whether it is coworkers or people who help with things like picking up food or our mail, feeding the dogs, gathering things, or helping out with the fundraising events. These are the behind-the-scenes friends who help keep you together. Without the support of friends, neighbors, family, and the town, our outcome would have been completely different. The network starts to grow to include people that know people. So, I guess do I accept that you are only given what you can handle to some extent, but it depends upon the individual as well as the kind of support network he or she has.

I believe in my heart we were lucky we lived in Norwood because there were so many people who came out of the woodwork to help us. I met people in Atlanta who suffered the same injury as Matt and were going home to rural Tennessee or rural Georgia with no support at all. They were going to face the same challenges and stress about quality of life and finances with no support. That's when I knew we were blessed.

People ask, "How can you consider yourself to be lucky? He's paralyzed." But the reality of it is that we are surrounded by so many people that care about him and that are going to help us get through this. It's the silver lining in it all. We have people calling us heroes and role models because we're showing people how to get through it. It's not, however, really that hard. You have to decide as a person and a family if you are going to deal with it positively or negatively. There's no real gray area in that regard. The medical end of it is more black and white, though. The staff don't want that gray area. When we all got excited when Matt wiggled his toes, the physical therapy staff said, "That's big, but it doesn't mean he can walk." You become very appreciative of the black-and-white aspect of it, so you don't get any false hopes. I am very proud that Matt, Kelley, Sue, and I decided we had only one choice, which was to face it head on. We don't piss and moan. We just try to make life the best it can be.

CHAPTER 19
We Will Move Forward; We Will Do This
By Sue Brown

Seeing Matt hit the boards and crumble to the ice took no more than a second, yet when I replay it in my head, it seems like the event lasted hours. I'm sure Matt's, Mike's, and my recollection of the actual event have melded with similar recaps because we've told and heard each other's version so many times.

In my recollection, Matt came off the bench and was heading towards the puck. It was down in the corner where we stood and came off the boards behind the net. Matt and Tyler were both racing for it. Matt was probably a split second ahead of Tyler, which would never have happened normally. Tyler was one of the fastest skaters around, Matt not so much. As they collided, Matt's momentum propelled him forward, and he ended up going headfirst into the boards.

It was immediately clear that something was really wrong. I started banging on the glass to get the ref's attention. I moved down to the door and stepped onto the ice, being told by the ref that I could not do that. I stepped off and then stepped back on, as everyone knew he was really hurt. At first they didn't allow Anne Cathcart, the nurse, on the ice until she could produce her nursing license. Not many nurses carry it with them, so eventually she was allowed on by the ref. If he hadn't allowed her, Matt may not be alive today.

Mike and I both got down in Matt's face and talked to him. He kept saying, "Mom, this is bad, this is really bad." I kept saying, "Let's just see what's going on." The paramedics and the Hingham Fire

Department did an unbelievable job. It took them forever to get him off the ice, but that's because they did it right. They didn't roll him until everyone was ready to roll him. They didn't take his helmet off, they unscrewed it. They clearly knew the second they arrived what they were dealing with.

Matt kept saying, "I can't feel anything, but it feels like my feet are in the air." I had a sense that this was a spinal cord injury. I stood on the ice, looking up and seeing all these people looking down. It seemed as though there were more people than there really were with all the eyes peering down at us. I went from feelings of, "I feel bad that we are holding up the game" back to, "I don't care. We are going to take as long as we need."

Then I realized that I needed to reach Kelley, who had been out with friends. I looked into the stands again, and it was evident that everyone was texting. I needed to get in touch with her so that she didn't hear about this through a mass of texts. I thought about my mother, who was gravely sick home with cancer. *Someone needs to let her know before anyone else hears and says something to her.* I went into mama-bear mode and was going to control anything and everything I could, because what was lying on the ice at my feet, I could not control. It's what gets me through situations like this. It's just my personality. I started texting as soon as I got into the ambulance and went through the mental checklist. I'm one of six kids and Mike is one of eight, so I made sure everyone heard that Matt had an accident. I was intent on feeding them the limited facts about what we knew and not innuendo and hearsay.

I texted my sister, who called back right away asking what I meant by "hurt badly." "Is he conscious?" she asked. I said, "Yes, but he can't move," so her first concern was his head. She immediately reached out to her boss, who happened to be in the Cayman Islands at a pediatric neurosurgeon conference with neurologists all over the world. She reached out to him as we were pulling into South Shore Hospital. He asked where they were taking him, and she said her guess was Boston

Children's Hospital. He said, "Wait a minute, I need to see who is here. If it's the spine I want to make sure the head neurosurgeon is there." The head trauma surgeon was at the conference, so that meant the head spine neurosurgeon was back in Boston. This was good news.

By the time we got to Boston Children's, Matt's CT scans were already in Grand Cayman being looked at by all the neurosurgeons there. When the neurosurgeon came in to see us, he said, "You know quite a few people. You won't believe how many calls I had last night from the Cayman Islands." So, by the next morning it really felt like everyone worldwide knew about Matt. I had also woken up to news of his injury on the TV and thought, *Are they talking about Matt?* The situation certainly took on a life of its own.

The ride to the hospital was painfully slow. I was fidgety, and the firefighter told me the ambulance would rock back and forth if went any faster. I never realized how many potholes there were coming out of the rink. When we hit one, the vehicle would jostle Matt, so the driver was going to go as slow as he could to minimize that.

As soon as I stepped out of the ambulance, I saw Lisa Gareri, who is a respiratory therapist from Norwood. I had an immediate sense of calm seeing someone I knew. She had heard it was a hockey player and came right down to South Shore. I was still in my take-charge mode and doing everything I could do in the trauma room. They saw that his oxygen stats were going down, so they decided they were going to need to put him on a respirator. They were hoping that the folks from Boston Children's were going to be there to do it, but they decided that they wanted to do it when everything was calm and collected, rather than if his oxygen started to plummet in the ambulance headed to Boston. We got to talk to Matt, and we took turns telling him everything was going to be all right and that we loved him. We let him know that he wasn't going to be able to talk when he first woke up. They gave him the medicine to put him to sleep so that they could intubate him. This was on a Saturday, and he woke up on Thursday, maybe even that Friday. In between, on Wednesday, they took him to

Boston Children's to stabilize his neck.

The group from Boston Children's arrived in their ambulance and in came Harriet, a nurse on the transport team. She either arrives in the helicopter or ambulance as the trauma nurse. She entered the ER, and I instantly fell in love with her. Matt immediately relaxed, even though he had those meds in him and was pretty sedated anyhow. A guy named Dave drove the ambulance, while I was texting and calling everyone. My cousin Peter was coaching Needham, and I reached out to him to let him know what was going on. He heard Matt was injured via the grape vine, which had reported that Matt broke his leg. How I wish it was his leg. Dave gave me some great words of wisdom that prepared me for what I was going to experience when we got to Boston Children's, and just hearing it was exactly what I needed. He told me there were going to be lots of people, since it is a teaching hospital. "Between the attendants, the residents, and the fellows, you're going to get a lot of people coming up to you." He even told me that the hospital chaplain would show up, and that was something I hadn't thought about. Knowing that the chaplain was to be expected made me feel a little easier, and it would stop me wondering if something was really wrong. He also told me about the social workers. When I got there, I was well prepared.

I was met by Dr. David Casavant. He was the critical care consultant on call that night. He kept coming over to us and telling what he was going to do, and I kept thinking, *Why? They just did all that stuff at South Shore. They're going to do all the scans again?* We went out to the waiting room. Mike kept saying he wanted them to come in and talk to us, but I did not. I already knew what the results were showing, and if I heard it, that made it real. Mike, on the other hand, needed to hear it to believe it.

Upon confirmation that it was indeed a spinal cord injury, we felt like we were the only ones going through it, and we were on an island by ourselves. However, we quickly realized how much support was out there for us. There were also a whole lot of people with spinal cord injuries, and even more who knew what we were going through.

That first night, it was kind of dark. We were wondering how we were going to do this and how we were going to afford it. We got way ahead of ourselves. I went into the room and made a comment about the future. That's when Dr. Casavant turned and said to me, "Relax, Mrs. Brown. Slow down, we'll talk about the future in the future, but right now Matt is not breathing on his own. He cannot stabilize his own blood pressure or body temperature. Right now he is fully dependent on life support. Let's get him through the night and we can worry about tomorrow, tomorrow. Right now we aren't going minute by minute, only hour by hour. He is not out of the woods yet. There are a lot of things that could go wrong, but there are a lot of things that can go right." That's when I realized just how big this injury was, yet he said it in a confident manner, so I wasn't afraid. I knew it would be okay in the long run. That's what you get being at Boston Children's, one of the best pediatric hospitals in the world. They were letting us know they were confident but it was real. It was serious, and was going to be a very long road. The phrase "it's a marathon not a sprint" was first uttered that night, and it definitely turned out to be a marathon.

Though not a very religious person, I grew up Catholic and decided that a prayer or two was in order. I began to pray, but then I got a bit angry. I thought if God really was a good, benevolent God, how could this happen to my little boy? A while later, a parish priest and friend of the family came in. When Chris Hickey came in, I told him I wasn't happy and that I wasn't happy with God. He assured me it was okay, that "He knows you're not happy." I slowly started to think there was a reason this happened. I realized I might not ever know why in my lifetime, but I came around to a belief that it happened to Matt for a reason.

A few months after the accident, we were talking to a father of one of Matt's buddies who shared with us that when he thinks of all of the boys on that team, he believed that Matt was the only one able to withstand and rise above it. Maybe there was a reason it had to happen on that night and during that game, but God decided he was the only kid who could handle it.

When Matt was in Atlanta, I would go down for a week while Mike worked and we would swap roles. I was down there one week, and I was just really sad and tired. We made the mistake of traveling on a Sunday, which meant you really had no downtime. You'd get home and into work on Monday. I was driving home from the hospital to the apartment and was really felt about to hit rock bottom. At that point, they were telling us he might never get off the respirator, and I was telling them that he would. That notion was the one thing I truly could not handle. That was the one thing I thought would change his life too much to bear. I cried myself to sleep at the thought that he would not be able to go out with his friends again.

I got to the Shepherd Center the next day, and there was a counselor there. She came up to me and said, "I want to show you something." We walked into Matt's room, and she said, "Okay, do it." He started to move his left arm. I thought to myself, *Okay, I am back.* When I truly felt at the point when I could not take it anymore, there was God, throwing me a little bone. "Here you go, Sue." Not that Matt has gotten his movement back, but I felt like this was God's way of showing us there is always hope on the horizon.

But even since day one at Boston Children's, Matt has set the pace. We have followed Matt. If Matt was sad, we were all sad. If Matt was happy, we were all happy. It was Matt who decided to suck it up and go after it. It was Matt who decided his life was not over, it had just changed. It was Matt who said, "I'm not crawling into a cocoon, so neither can you." We follow his lead. I give him all the credit. People have said, "Well, you did it, too." I believe I did what every parent would do because I love my children and try to do what's best for them. But this is all Matt. I might have crawled into a cocoon. I might have said, "This isn't fair. I don't want this." It was Matt who said, "We will go forward. We will do this."

That is not to say he doesn't need reminding of this every once in a while. Eight or nine months after the accident, I was getting him ready for physical therapy and tying his shoes. I was standing at the end of his bed looking at him, and he said, "I don't want to do this anymore."

I said, "What don't you want to do?"

"I don't want to do this anymore. I don't want to be paralyzed," he said.

I looked at him and said, "You have the same two choices you had when you first got hurt. Whenever you hit a plateau or a wall, you can either move forward or give up. Those are the same two options you had."

He looked back at me and said, "Fine. I'll go to PT. I'll keep moving forward."

We've had similar conversations when I said he had to suck it up. We had one at Boston Children's. Matt became very sensitive to noise when he was first admitted. At first, he had two nurses to take care of the machines, and then there was one nurse who would never leave his room. But as he got better, there was one nurse who would visit while doing rounds, which meant Matt had to wait a little bit. He was getting agitated one night when the IV machine was beeping. I said to him, "You know what, Buttercup? You need to suck it up and wait because you are no longer the sickest person on the floor." My sister, who was visiting at the time and party to the conversation, was taken aback at first, but then said, "That was just what he needed to hear. He is no longer the sickest person." That's when you get the ability to move forward; when you realize it could be worse, and you don't have to look very far at Boston Children's to realize that. We got to take him home, and he's going to live a strong and healthy life. There were other parents in the ICU who cannot say the same about their kid.

A major life-changing event in Matt's recovery was the entrance into our world of Wesley Burhoe. Matt worked really hard that first summer to get caught up with his classes so he could enter junior year with his friends. (A bit of that might have had to do with not wanting to graduate with his little sister.) Nevertheless, we needed someone to help him navigate the hallways, take notes, and do his classwork. The agency told us that they were sending over a man to introduce himself as a candidate for the position. When I opened the front door, Wes was just bigger than life. He is 6'7" and built like a football player. He is as wide as he is tall and strong. All I can describe Wes as is a gentle giant.

Matt focused on returning to school to be with his buddies, while all I thought about was his safety. As a mother, it's about the what-ifs. What if there is a fire? What if Matt needs to get out? I conveyed my concerns to Wes and he said to me, "We have gone over the protocol if there's a fire. We will stay put, and the fire department will come to us." I knew it was unlikely that anything would happen, but I thought, *What if there's smoke? You're telling my baby to stay put?* Wes must have sensed that when he said, "Oh, if there is smoke we are leaving."

I said, "Okay, good. Scoop him up, throw him over your shoulder and leave the chair. The chair is not important."

Wes took a step back and sized Matt up in the chair. "How much does Matt weigh?" he asked.

"I don't know … 115 pounds?" I said.

"How much does the chair weigh?"

I said, "350 pounds, maybe."

Wes nodded and said very calmly, "We will get both of them. Don't worry, Mrs. Brown. I have his back. We'll be fine."

He was young, so I knew he would fit in with Matt and his friends, but his calm confidence was a big selling point that provided me with the assurance that we would be okay. For that short period of time, confidence was exactly what Matt needed, and we owe lots of thanks to Wes for being in Matt's life.

Matt's friends, like many groups, have a bunch of different personalities: some who think things through and some who jump in with both feet and don't worry that it's the deep end. During that first summer, the boys wanted to go to the movies. Mike wanted to show them how to clear Matt's trach tube. When Mike asked, "Who wants to learn?" a few said, "Nope, no thanks, not me." While a couple said, "Yes, I got this. Show me how." A few even said, "Yep. You don't even need to show me. I got this."

None of them were driving at that time, so I was the chauffeur. We arrived at the movies, and the boys jumped out of the car. I told one of Matt's friends I was running across the street to my office and could be back in three minutes if he needed me. After a couple hours, they texted that they were ready. As I was pulling up, they were just getting ready to suction Matt's tube and I saw Brendan kneeling down and getting all the stuff he was going to need. He put his supplies on the ground, including the catheter that was going to go into Matt's neck. He brushed his hands-off, then took his two fingers and wiped off the catheter. He suctioned him out, put the button back on the tube, and jumped in the car. I didn't say anything because I knew more important than the tube being sterile, Matt needed to be with those boys. I realized then that he would be okay being with them if he were choking or needed to clear something he couldn't. There are no rocks in his lungs, so we were good. Everything that we said to do was done, just in sixteen-year-old-boy style.

I spend countless hours thinking about Matt's future, and I think that the future holds whatever Matt wants it to hold. I think the advancements in spinal cord research are what will determine a portion of the future, but not everything. I do believe they are making big gains. They are starting to do some things with nerve transplants, allowing people to do more with their arms. For Matt, the most difficult part is going to be waiting for the new treatments. Matt would kill for the use of his arms. He might not even ask for full mobility, but he would really love the use of his arms back. You have to be careful about doing one thing that precludes you from doing others as progress continues. I do believe that with the spinal cord research they are doing, he will get some great use soon and that will open many more doors.

The first time I saw him standing and walking in a sling was over

over at Journey Forward, an activity-based therapy center in Canton, Massachusetts. It was unbelievable. Matt went to the Shepherd Center, which is world renowned, and they didn't even have one of these machines. We went to this little outpatient PT place in Canton that people don't even know about and saw all the equipment they had, and it made me wonder why a place like Shepherd doesn't have one of these for every patient. Why couldn't he be on it from day one, when they first stood him up? Seeing him standing really took my breath away. I thought I might never see that. I understand it was assisted, but seeing the look on his face and in his eyes when he saw himself in the mirror, took my breath away. I think it would take my breath away to see his arms start working. I think that's what hurts the most is just wanting a hug, so when he gets that ability to use his arms back, the first thing I want—and this is selfish of me—is a hug.

When Matt was getting out of the Shepherd Center, my sister-in-law, Nancy, and I went over to Boston Medical Center and met Steve Williams, a psychiatrist of physical medicine and rehab doctor. He was doing the spinal cord care over there. I don't like to talk to these people because once I do it makes it real again. But we walked out after speaking with him, and all I could think was, *Oh my God. I love Steve Williams. I can't wait for Matt to meet him and start going to see him.* We left there and went directly over to Journey Forward to check out the facility. We walked into Journey Forward, and I thought, *I can really see Matt going here.* At Shepherd, everything felt very sterile. He couldn't get on one of the bikes because they would have to lift him out of his chair. At Journey Forward, they just take the foot plates off his chair and wheel him right up. It looks more like a YMCA gym then a hospital, and so Matt can simply work out with his buddies like he would have at the regular gym. Journey Forward is now bursting at the seams. They have hired many more people and now have longer hours to accommodate the demand.

I think back to a time when I had thought there was no one out there who understood what we were going through. Now I realize there is a whole world of people out there who understand. There was a family who moved in right across the street from us, a young family, that was always very supportive. One day we got a call telling us that their nephew had been in a car accident and was paralyzed. We talked to them about what we went through and what worked and what didn't. We have stayed close to them, and now their son Mark goes to Journey Forward. Another time, I was in Charleston, SC, and received a call from Dr. Casavant telling us a relative of his suffered a spinal injury. That's why I always say we are here for anyone going through it too and wants to talk.

Matt has become good friends with Nick Malafronte from Abington who was hurt in a fall. His dad, Vic, called me when Nick first got hurt. He said, "You don't know me, but I heard your story and was wondering if Matt would reach out to Nick." I got home and told Matt. He looked at me and said, "Let's go right now." So into Boston we went during rush hour. Matt wheeled right into Nick's room at the hospital, and they started chitchatting and have been buddies ever since. Nick now also goes to Journey Forward.

I went up to Nick's mom to talk, and I almost giggled because I looked into her eyes and saw what I must have looked like at that same point in time. Whenever a doctor came into talk to us about Matt, and I all I heard was "Wah, wah, wah." I could not understand the words that she was saying because I was just so tired and so emotional. When I looked at Nick's mom, I said, "I know exactly this feeling. You do not even hear what I am saying." We still laugh about it to this day.

There are two other memorable moments that make me cry every time I relive them. My mother, who was diagnosed with cancer in the fall of 2009, was told she probably would not make it through Christmas because her cancer was very aggressive. We got through the holidays and then took her to the doctor. He said, "Any day now. Just be prepared it could be any day." Matt had his accident at the end of January, and my mother, who was pretty confused before his accident, was thrown over the edge. I went to visit, and she was holding a picture of Matt to her chest. She said to me, "Did you hear about the boy down the street?" I told her I had. She asked, "Do you think he's going to be okay?" I said, "Yes, he's getting stronger every day." She was hugging and kissing the picture and kept calling him the boy down the street because I think her mind wasn't allowing he to go there. She came in to visit him at Boston Children's and immediately kissed him and hugged him. We went down to Atlanta, and she became sicker and sicker. My sister called me and said, "I don't think Mom is going to make it. She is wasting away and spending a lot of time sleeping." I told Matt, and he turned to me and said with such conviction, "No, it's okay. She will be there when I get home." When it then came time to decide when Matt was going to be discharged, he kept saying he wanted to come home on May fifth. I said, "Okay, we will tidy everything up in these next two weeks and shoot for May fifth." Around this time my older sister was at my mother's house preparing for my parents wedding anniversary on April twenty-fourth. My sister said to Mom, "You have a big day coming up." My mom said, "Yep, May fifth." No one knew what the significance of May fifth was. Nobody knew then that was the day Matt was coming home. My sister said to her, "No, Mom, April twenty-fourth was the day you and Dad got married." Mom kept saying, "May fifth is the big day."

We came home, and Matt flew in to Norwood Airport. He was picked up by the Norwood Fire Department who took him first to my mother's house. My mother got out of bed and walked down the hall to kiss him. She turned and went back down the hall into bed. She died a week later. As angry as I was at God when Matt first had his accident, I thanked him for that. I could not have dealt with her dying, me being in Atlanta, Matt being in Atlanta, and having to deal with everything. She waited for him to come home. They both decided on that date.

The final story I'd like to share shows what a very caring and compassionate young man Matt is. One morning at Boston Children's,

I heard the click of his mouth making it clear that he wanted to talk. He asked, "Why me?" I said I didn't know but thought there was a reason, we just didn't know it yet. I shared what Mr. Dolan said: "Maybe it is just because you are the strongest one on the team. The one who could best handle it."

He asked, "Will I ever walk again?"

I said, "I don't know, but no one on the floor said you wouldn't and we will just keep moving forward."

He wrapped up our brief Q and A session by asking, "Is the boy from Weymouth okay?"

It makes me cry to this day because, even as an adult, I'm not sure that I would've cared much to go there. But Matt cared about Tyler. He does care, and he cares about everybody, so he will be okay. I told him that I had seen Tyler at a hockey game. I introduced myself and told him we would continue to follow him and his career. Tyler told me he wasn't sure if he was going to continue playing hockey. I told him, "Yes, you are. You are a good hockey player and you need to." The way that accident affected both boys' lives makes me cry to this day. Both of them have turned out just fine, but the emotions that this accident stirred up was a lot for any boy to have handled. I'm confident, though, that the world is a better place as a result of their experience.

For now, Matt is going back to school for his masters, and hopefully that helps him find a career that he enjoys. It's about taking another step outside his comfort zone. He did college, but he hesitated in finding that next thing. He just can't pop in his car and go to work. He's going to need someone there with him. When a company hires him, they're going to be hiring someone else to support him. Companies would need to make some accommodations for him. Legally they have to, but he does not want anyone to feel forced to, so he does not want to push that. I think something with the NHL or a job in marketing or scouting would be ideal. He really sees the game differently and studies it. He would be very productive, but it's all about getting his foot in the door.

CHAPTER 20
Why Me!

"Bad things do happen; how I respond to them defines my character and the quality of my life. I can choose to sit in perpetual sadness, immobilized by the gravity of my loss, or I can choose to rise from the pain and treasure the most precious gift I have—life itself."

— **Walter Anderson**

So, what does it all mean? Why did all of this happen and, especially, why did it happen to me? Today, I don't know for sure, though I'm fairly confident I'll learn the answer at some point. Regarding religion, I'm not certain what I believe, but I do feel that at some point we are all made privy to where we fit into the big equation. I find it difficult to fathom that we are all mutually exclusive beings, plopped on the planet, without any predestined plan for who we meet and what occurs during our journey. That just seems a bit too arbitrary and left to chance. Instead, I feel that we all have individual reasons for being and for encountering the people and the situations that are placed before us. This concept helps me not only make sense of my injury but it also helps answer the unanswerable question of why bad things happen to good people. My mom shares with me often what

Mr. Dolan believes; that there was no one else on the team that could have handled it. Was it through my selection as the sacrificial lamb that others will benefit somewhere down the line?

I do believe that as a result of my injury, I've learned some very valuable lessons and perhaps sharing those lessons with others is the greatest gift that I can provide. Never go to bed mad, and use every opportunity you're granted to say I love you and appreciate the world as you know it. I'm not a philosopher and will never be able to answer the question why me? If the sacrifice of my physical abilities helps to teach others lessons in patience and compassion, in love and strength and perseverance, then it is a good trade to make. I am just one kid, who experienced a devastating loss, but through my loss, I have been granted the ability to enhance the lives of others. I'll make that trade any day of the week. It's taken me a while to understand and accept this.

If I were able to turn back time and count one, two, and three (ironically the date of my injury, January 23), things would play out as follows:

> Hoping to produce the lift the team needed, I jumped the boards fired up, intent on doing just what Coach Clifford ordered. Our bench was on the other end of the rink, so I gained speed as I chased the puck towards our defensive zone. I felt like the entire bench had their eyes on me, knowing that I wanted to make something happen. From a hockey standpoint, I was totally out of position as a forward, behind our own net, but I was a bit embarrassed about the way we played and the way I played in the first period, and was hell bent on making up for it. I was hoping that my hustle would provide a spark to elevate our game.
>
> I gathered the puck in somewhere around the face-off dot, and as I was circling around the net, the puck came off my stick and ricocheted off the end board. As it bounced off the back

wall, it nestled between my feet. I looked down to regain control of the wobbling puck and felt a Weymouth player converge on me. He bumped me from behind, not a vicious hit, just a bump. I kept my head up, as my dad had always taught me, and braced myself against the boards. My dad and mom, who don't usually stand together at the game, were just beyond the glass watching as I side-stepped Tyler. I smirked quickly at them, my biggest fans, and shot the puck down the half wall.

Obviously, I would have been content if such a momentous hockey play had unfolded with a more positive outcome. Or would I? What if, I had handled the puck cleanly and made an insignificant clearing pass down the far wall? I would have probably remained a third-line varsity winger on the Norwood Mustangs hockey team. My fantasy stat line closing out my three-year varsity career would have likely read somewhere in the vicinity of four goals, eight assists, and twenty-one penalty minutes, and included an historic game-winning goal against rival Walpole in the final game of my senior year. I can safely assume that jersey "3" would have never been retired and would have been worn by a long list of Norwood High hockey hopefuls for many generations to come.

I would have graduated from Norwood High with a B–C average and would have appeared in the yearbook listed as class clown and most likely to accomplish mediocrity. After an uneventful four-year college experience at Stonehill, where I drank too much and studied too little, I'd have graduated as Magna Cum Unremarkable and faced a stack of student loans sure to haunt me for the next twenty years.

If I fantasize a bit more, I can fast-forward to my fairly meaningless job that I go to every day for the next forty-seven years before retiring at age sixty-five, wondering if the successor to Social Security will still be around for my kids … mine and Meghan's, of course.

I'd read about Tyler Piacentini, the kid I sidestepped in a game on January 23, 2010. Tyler would go on to play hockey at Norwich

University before playing some semi-pro hockey. He might often think about the slick move that Brown kid made in that game against Norwood several years earlier.

Mom and Dad would grow old together. Kelley might still have become a nurse but may have lacked the compassion that is required to become successful in the medical field. Grandma would have still passed away when she decided it was time but without worrying about what happened to that boy down the street. My buddies Austin, Ty, Mark, Pete, Kyle, and Rob would have shared some good times together, drank some beers, and unfortunately grown apart as all adults usually do.

There still would have been a Travis Roy, a Dennis Doherty, a Lucas Carr, a Wesley Burhoe, a Pat Lee, an Anton Clifford, or even that cute Italian nurse I puked on at South Shore, but none of them would be a part of my life. I would have never run the Boston Marathon (I can assure you) and would have been very unlikely to kiss the Stanley Cup with Ference, hang out with Zdeno Chara, had a Canadian Olympic gold medal draped around my neck, or worn the army ranger jacket that helped guide the Bruins to the Stanley Cup. I would not have had Patrice Bergeron to call my friend or have dropped the puck at center ice of the TD Garden before thousands of inspired fans.

And that's the key word to my story. Inspired.

Had I simply picked up the puck and flipped it over the head of the oncoming opponent, I would have missed out on the opportunity to inspire. Sometimes, I am amazed that my story has inspired so many, yet I know in my heart that through strength, courage, and perseverance, I've been able to encourage others to overcome obstacles. Through my absolute commitment to my Never Quit mantra, many have been inspired to face their own tragedies head on and have chosen to never quit. Through hard work and faith that medical technology is within striking distance of allowing me to regain movement of my arms, my legs, or both, my story is inspiring others.

I hope that through my sacrifice and my decision to remain

positive, others who may have given up on themselves choose to remain resilient and turn their backs on failure, pressing forward no matter how insurmountable the odds may seem. It's through that belief that I can begin to understand the reason things happened as they did, and instead of asking, "Why Me?" I am beginning to know why me!

The world is filled with some very disturbing events these days. One can't sit and watch the evening news without questioning what our planet is coming to and whether or not this was the intention when the Big Plan was masterminded. I'm not of the illusion that my recovery or my inspiration alone is going to make much of a difference to the big picture. I do, however, believe that my decision to keep pressing forward in a positive manner can have an impact on a few who are able to learn of my story, to hear me speak, or to read this book. I've already made a positive impact in many lives and hope that my complete recovery will make a substantive contribution into the recovery of others. That is what makes this entire ordeal, this entire journey, all worth it.

From the time I was at Boston Children's, I realized how many people were cheering me on and rooting for me. I realized that giving up would not only be letting myself down, but so many who had pinned their hopes on my wellbeing. I was only fifteen at the time, but I committed to working as hard as I could for as long as it takes to bring my recovery to the finish line. To this point, it's been eight long years, and I still wait each morning for my parents to enter my room to get me out of bed. I sit in a wheelchair each day and spend hours maneuvering through my own personal challenges, and I am essentially no closer to being healed then I was eight years ago. Nonetheless, my hope remains strong because recovery becomes more and more real every day. I will push myself every day until a cure is at hand. The day that I give up and relegate myself to another sixty years in a chair is the day that I believe that a cure is no longer possible. I'm not certain if the cure will be through regeneration of my nerves at the point where my injury occurred, or if there will be the invention of a device that will simulate my spinal cord, but I truly believe that the reality of a full recovery is just over the horizon.

My paralysis is no longer the equivalent of a death sentence as it once was for so many. Doctors no longer have the unenviable task of telling spinal cord injury survivors that they will never walk again. Medical science has made such amazing progress, and I am committed to continuing everything I do in order keep my body healthy and a viable candidate for a cure.

A close friend of mine, Matt Curran, suffered a spinal cord injury and has been able to get his mobility back. Matt, a former hockey player at Providence College, fell three stories from a building and was told he could never walk again. Today, you would barely even know he was once injured. Matt regained mobility and was able to walk again on his own. Today, he continues his recovery with fine motor training and has completed the 5K Ruckus Run. He is working on his balance and has recently found a passion for boxing. During one of our first meetings, he told me what kept him going and talked about the question, "What if?" What if tomorrow is the day? What if tomorrow my arms and legs wake up? What if tomorrow is the day a message gets through from my brain and my arms and legs receive it? What if tomorrow is the day a cure is discovered? Why would I ever stop trying if tomorrow could be that day? With that in mind, failing to continue will never be an option.

I currently try to keep my body as flexible as possible by working out three days a week for two hours a day. Though I enjoy a few drinks now and then, I'm not destroying my body with alcohol or drugs. I keep my muscles as strong as possible. I go to Journey Forward in Canton, just a few miles from my house. Canton is essentially in my backyard, which is a blessing because other clients come from as far as Maine, New Hampshire, and even from other countries to benefit from the programs Journey Forward has to offer spinal cord injury survivors. When I'm there, I stand and take steps in a machine that is guiding me. I stimulate my muscles every session as part of the neural recovery network which allows them to remain strong.

Journey Forward founder and a spinal cord injury survivor Dan Cummings left Boston to rehab at Project Walk in San Diego. He began his rehab in a wheelchair but walked out three years later with just the help of a walker. He founded Journey Forward after realizing that he had to leave Boston, the mecca of the healthcare field, to find a suitable rehab place on the other side of the country. Journey Forward is focused on providing the most advanced care possible and is part of the Reeve Foundation's NeuroRecovery Network®, established by Christopher and Dana Reeve. This association of recovery centers provides data from training sessions to medical researchers studying paralysis and working to make rehabilitation techniques more effective.

One of the things that keeps me journeying forward is seeing Dan and all the others who have gotten function back. Another motivator is the continued support from the community and the nonstop messages I receive from supporters who still have my back through it all. Lastly, I accept that I have just one life to live and that is precious. I am not going to stop until I squeeze every last bit of juice out of this precious fruit called life.

I encourage high school students and anyone who hears me speak to lean on others when you need to and to reciprocate to others when they are in need. My lesson is to live each day like it's your last, because you can't fathom how quickly life as you know it can be snatched away before the end of your next shift.

Our current and future goal of getting the Matt Brown Foundation, off the ground is also close to becoming a reality. We are about to push the paperwork through to make us an official 501(c)(3). Once that occurs we can begin raising money and putting it to good use. There are so many people out there who aren't as fortunate as I am. There are people who couldn't afford to get their house refitted or purchase the proper bed or machines. Their bills are through the roof. That's where the Matt Brown Foundation hopes to assist, in much the same way as the Boston Bruins Foundation stepped in to help me with my chair and the Travis Roy Foundation helped me with my first van. I want to be there to help people with their needs in much the same way.

If all of this comes to fruition, which I'm confident that it will, I'll be able to look back at my life and consider it a huge victory. The ability to help others in need, even through your own personal sacrifice, is the greatest gift that anyone can give. I don't think that the previous version of myself, the pre-injury version would likely feel the same, but the present-day Matt certainly does.

I may never again see my name on another hockey stat sheet, but the next goal I score will be that of moving my arms and taking a single step under my own power.

My next assist will be helping others who need my inspiration or financial help.

My next power play will be to rise from my chair and thank my parents, my sister, my friends, family and supporters for never giving up on me and providing me with the strength and will to Never Quit.

And my final empty netter, the score that will mean more to me than the game-winning goal I was never able to experience, will be walking over to my parents, standing tall, looking my dad in the eye and shaking his hand, and giving mom that hug she so greatly deserves. And there won't be a dry eye in the crowd.

AFTERWORD

By Pat Lee

I played basketball at Stonehill College and graduated in 2012. After graduation, I took a job coaching the men's basketball team as a graduate assistant. Stonehill had agreed to pay for my classes after I received my degree in Athletics Administration from Endicott College, but I needed to make some extra money in order to pay rent, buy pizza, and to have a bit of spare change in my pocket.

As luck would have it, the job I stumbled upon was worth far more to me than a large deep-dish pepperoni. I become an aide for the incomparable Matt Brown during his academic career at Stonehill. More than his aide, I became his friend and was provided with so much more than I could have ever provided for Matt. In many ways, I should have paid him because spending time with him enhanced my life in countless ways.

I had known Matt's Aunt Trish, the head women's basketball coach at Stonehill, for a few years. Trish approached me with the opportunity to work with Matt. She briefed me on his injury and advised me that he needed help around campus. I was very interested and met Matt and his dad, Mike, right before the school year started. We instantly connected, and I gratefully accepted the role.

My duties were nothing very difficult and included bringing him to and from classes, feeding him his meals, and helping him get to any meetings he had on campus. I drove him to and from physical therapy at Journey Forward in Canton three days a week. There were also many intangibles that don't get listed in the job description, things like making sure he was comfortable in his chair, scratching anywhere that may have an itch, wiping his nose and, all in all, being his right hand, his left hand, and both legs. Our ability to read each other grew to the point that he would just look at me without saying a word and I knew what he needed. We developed a pretty close connection.

Witnessing Matt's life on a daily basis made me a better human being, and it is safe to say that anyone who has met him leaves with a very similar feeling. I'd describe Matt as strong, kind, considerate, and determined. There are very few in his situation who would be nearly as positive and continue to live as fulfilling a life as he does. It comes down to attitude, and Matt simply refuses to let negativity creep into his mind. He puts others' needs before his own, which is a credit to him considering the daily challenges he faces. I'm extremely confident that he will be rewarded for his selflessness and his forever-positive approach to life.

His motto is "Never Quit," and he lives by this every moment of every day. He has not wavered from day one, and he is constantly working both mentally and physically to achieve his end goal of walking again. I know he will accomplish this, and I cannot wait for that day to be upon us.

I have developed an equally close relationship with his family. His parents have been especially generous to me and often invite me to events, as if I'm the Brown that no one ever talks about. There is always a couch available if one of our evenings runs a little later than expected.

I have grown immensely as a person while working with Matt. He is so easy going and does not let anything get him down. It is difficult to worry about my own tiny problems after witnessing the challenges he faces daily with a smile. If the world had more Matt Browns, what a wonderful world it would be.

ACKNOWLEDGMENTS

To my family, friends, and those who have continued to support me since day one—I truly cannot thank you enough. I could try to name everyone by name, but I know I would inadvertently leave someone out. Although this journey has taken longer than I had hoped, longer than I had expected, you all have made each and every day easier with your smiles, words of encouragement, and well wishes.